Looking Back

Looking Back

THE AMERICAN DREAM
THROUGH IMMIGRANT EYES

Marie Jastrow

INTRODUCTION BY
Robert Jastrow

W.W. NORTON & CO., INC.
NEW YORK   LONDON

Library of Congress Cataloging-in-Publication Data

Jastrow, Marie.
Looking Back.

1. Jastrow, Marie.   2. New York (N.Y.)—
Biography.   3. United States—Emmigration and immigra-
tion—Biography.
I. Title.
F128.9.J5J37 1986   974.7'1004924 (B)   86-8762
ISBN 0-393-02348-6

Published in Canada by Penguin Books, Canada Ltd.,
2801 John Street, Markham, Ontario L3R 1B4.
Printed in the United States of America.

W. W. Norton and Co., Inc., 500 Fifth Avenue
New York, N.Y. 10110
W. W. Norton and Co. Ltd., 37 Great Russell
Street, London WC1B 3NU

Looking Back

Contents

INTRODUCTION
A Nation of Nations

*M*ore than a million and a quarter immigrants came to America in the memorable year of 1907 — the year in which my mother came from Germany to join my grandfather in New York City. Thousands arrived at Ellis Island every day in that year; on one April day, 11,745 new Americans entered through the Golden Door. In some instances, whole villages emigrated to the United States. The mayor of an Italian village is said to have welcomed a visiting dignitary with the words, "I greet you in the name of four thousand citizens, three thousand of whom are in America."

All told, thirty-three million immigrants came to the United States from Europe in the years leading up to the first World War. This great movement of European peoples to America began with the emigration of the British, Irish, Germans and Scandinavians and gradually shifted its focus to Italy, the Balkans and central Europe. Across the Atlantic went nearly nine million Americans-to-be from Britain and Ireland, six million from Germany, two million from Sweden and Norway, five million from Italy, three million from the Balkans, and eight million from Austria-Hungary, Poland and Russia.

Why did these tens of millions leave their homeland to come to America? Economic opportunity was a part of the answer. One Hungarian immigrant wrote, "I work from six in the morning until seven at night and get $10-$11 a week. . . . At home I made that much money in a whole month."

But money was not the whole story. Many Europeans were attracted by the democratic nature of American society, by its unstuffy ways, and its informality. Their delighted recognition of American egalitarianism appears again and again in immigrant letters.

"My cap is not worn out from raising it in the presence of gentlemen" . . . "The shoemaker and the teacher have the same title — 'mister'" . . . "By their dress, you could not tell a bank president from his office boy" . . . "[Even] if you are a millionaire you are called a 'mister' . . ."

My grandfather took great pleasure in the simplicity of American ways, the casual manners, the lack of pomp. I remember that he liked to take off his coat, tie and collar and sit by the window reading the *Staats-Zeitung*. If visitors came to the door, he welcomed them in his shirtsleeves and suspenders. That would be unthinkable in the old country.

Opapa particularly liked the American disregard for class distinction, the acceptance of people for what they were, no matter what they did for a living. When my grandfather first came to this country he was unable to find a job, his main work experience in Europe having been running several small businesses that failed. As his situation grew increasingly hopeless, he wanted to write to his in-laws in Serbia, but he was too proud to admit that he had failed again. Finally he collapsed of hunger and exhaustion outside a large building downtown on the East Side, which turned out to be St. Mark's Hospital. The staff took him in, fed him, gave him a mop, and Opapa had his first job in the promised land — porter.

In Europe, a job mopping floors would have been a terrible humiliation for a businessman. But Opapa did not mind. He was hungry, and besides — this was America, a land where, as another immigrant wrote, "Honest labor is no disgrace."

Unlike some immigrants, my grandfather never became rich in America; he never found the streets that were paved with gold; but he loved the American life.

After the Great War, my grandmother crossed the ocean again to see her parents, who had lost their home and suffered considerably in the fighting that raged across Serbia, but my grandfather refused to go with her. He had had enough of Europe. He never went back.

Perhaps the most powerful attraction of all for the European immigrant was the fact that Americans placed more value on ability than on birth. Word had come back to the old country that in America humble origins were no barrier to wealth and high status. Michael Pupin, who became a distinguished member of the faculty of Columbia University, came alone to this country from Serbia at the age of fifteen, with five cents in his pocket. His mother and father could neither read nor write and most of the people in his native town were illiterate. But in America the doors of the institutions of higher learning were open to a talented individual, and even to a penniless immigrant, if he worked hard enough.

Michael Pupin carried coal from sidewalks into cellars at fifty cents a ton, shovelled snow, painted basements and worked in a boiler room. At times he survived on five-cent meals of bean soup and bread. It is hard to say when he slept. He spent his nights studying engineering in free classes at Cooper Union, boned up on Greek and Latin to pass the entrance exams for Columbia College, memorized the first two books of the Iliad and four orations of Cicero, and made a profound impression on the Columbia professors who examined him. They awarded him a full tuition scholarship.

Pupin went on to become a great inventor and an eminent scientist. When I studied for my Ph.D. degree in theoretical physics at Columbia University, my classes and laboratories were held in a building named after the distinguished Columbia professor who had come to New York as a poor immigrant many years before.

One of Michael Pupin's inventions solved the problem of long distance telephoning. At the time, distant cities could not be connected by telephone because signals weakened so rapidly as they flowed along the wires. But armed with the "Pupin coil", a product of Pupin's ingenuity, telephone engineers built telephone lines that carried messages across the entire continent. AT&T told Pupin that without his invention the company would have spent the equivalent of many more billions of additional dollars to wire up the United States. Efficient, low-cost telephone service — the nervous system of the entire American economy — was this immigrant's way of paying back the country that had taken him in and given him the opportunity to realize his potential greatness.

Opportunity awaited the immigrant with Pupin's talent and energy, but first he had to get here. Immigrants at the turn of the century had to suffer much on the passage to America. This was not a journey for the physically weak, the faint-hearted or the irresolute. Pupin wrote later, "He who has never crossed the stormy Atlantic in the crowded steerage of immigrant ships does not know what hardships are."

Pupin had sold his books and sheepskin coat to raise the fare for the passage, having seen pictures of nearly naked Indians, and reasoning that the United States must be a very warm country where coats would not be needed. Then, when he reached the port of Hamburg and paid for his passage, he had no money left to buy a blanket and mattress for his steerage bunk. The voyage took place in the stormy month of March, with icy winds sweeping through the ship. It was bitter cold — too cold to stay in a bare bunk without coat or blanket, and Pupin hugged the ship's smokestack at night to keep from freezing to death.

When Pupin arrived in New York and confessed to the immigration officials that he had five cents in his pocket, no relatives in America and no training in a craft, they nearly sent him back. If they had, Pupin wrote later, "I should not be among the living." To face the hardships of the steerage passage with hope in one's heart was one thing; to return in the same dreadful conditions with only despair for company was another. Fear of being deported gripped the heart of every immigrant. Most, like Pupin, had cut their ties and sold all they owned to raise the money for the voyage. Now, within sight of the promised land, they might be turned away to face poverty and disgrace in the old country.

For many, it was more than the human spirit could bear. Over the course of the years, some immigrants jumped into the cold waters of the bay and tried to swim ashore, and others committed suicide rather than be

Michael Pupin in his senior year at Columbia.

Albert Einstein and Charles Steinmetz (*opposite*)—two great scientists who emigrated to America. Einstein needs no introduction. Steinmetz, genius of the General Electric Company, made alternating current machinery possible. His work introduced the Age of Electricity in American industry.

Steinmetz, born physically handicapped, arrived in the United States with $10, no job and no knowledge of English. He was about to be deported when a traveling companion produced a large amount of cash and said it belonged to them both. How fortunate it is for America that this man was admitted and could give his talents to the United States.

deported. Only one percent of those who arrived at Ellis Island were turned back, but that was one percent out of ten million Europeans who came to the United States in the peak period of immigration. One percent of ten million is one hundred thousand men and women — one hundred thousand tragedies, one hundred thousand souls condemned to despair.

What manner of individual would undertake a venture so arduous and uncertain as this? These were brave souls who left behind family, friends, every vestige of their old life, and undertook the terrible steerage passage with no assurance that they could even set foot on American soil at the end of their voyage. That is not a gamble everyone would make.

The Europeans who set out for America must have been a rare breed of men and women to risk all they had on such a journey into the unknown. And, in fact, it is the case that although poverty and oppression afflicted most of the workers and peasants of Europe, only one in ten came to America. The majority stayed behind. Few could bring themselves to make the fateful decision to leave their homes; most preferred to retain the emotional comfort of their traditional lifestyle, even at the cost of impoverishment.

It has always been so in the history of life. When adverse forces press upon a population and survival becomes increasingly difficult, only the venturesome few seek their opportunities in a new environment. The bonds of habit are strong in the human animal.

I believe these circumstances may explain the special traits of the American personality that are frequently remarked upon by the rest of the world. Why is the typical American less bound by tradition, more impatient of constraints, more independent-minded than almost anyone else? Why is he more innovative, more entrepreneurial, quicker to adopt new fashions and quicker still to discard them?

Perhaps the reason is that we are nearly all immigrants or descended from immigrants. There are few among us whose parents or grandparents did not have to struggle to reach these shores. From the Mayflower to the Vietnamese boat people, we Americans are of a rugged stock of men and women who came to this country from distant lands in journeys exhausting, painful and fraught with risk. Perhaps the very act of immigration itself, by its arduous and unpredictable nature, has culled from the peoples of the world those individuals of a bold and adventurous outlook, who were willing to take risks for the promise of great rewards.

"To immigrate is an entrepreneurial act," says Professor Edward Roberts of MIT. In this analogy between the immigrant and the entrepreneur may lie the secret of the American personality, and of America's economic growth and prosperity as well. In today's world, in which the productivity of human labor is augmented at a breathtaking pace by technological innovations, the wealth of nations resides more in their human capital — the brains and energy of their people — than in the diamonds, gold and oil their lands may yield. "The productivity of human labor" is a dry term, but it is the key to the strength of America. The wealth of an oil-rich nation comes out of the ground and can run dry. The wealth of an entrepreneurial nation comes from the brains of its people, and is potentially inexhaustible.

The open society of America, its upward mobility, the kudos it bestows on the risk taker, the great rewards available to the successful inventor and businessman through the liquidity of our capital markets — all these give free rein and encouragement to the creative and innovative energies of the human being. It was just those qualities of American society that drew such men as Michael Pupin and my grandfather to our shores. Some, like Michael Pupin, who were favored with exceptional talent, enterprise, and luck, achieved wealth and distinction. Others, like my grandfather, remained in obscurity.

But it can be said of all that they brought with them to these shores the priceless qualities of persistence, hard work and entrepreneurial energy, through which they have contributed to the greatness of America out of proportion to their numbers.

Robert Jastrow
December 1985

20

Looking Back

1
To America

My parents came from the Serbian town called Yarac, in a remote corner of the globe now known as Yugoslavia. When my father decided to see the world at the age of fourteen, he took his leave from his parents without their consent and departed. He must have been content with his adventure because he stayed away, and at the age of eighteen he landed in the city of Zurich in Switzerland. There he found his haven in a Swiss bookstore.

Ten years later, he spread his wings once again to leave for his hometown in Serbia. In Yarac, he met and married my mother, the daughter of a well-to-do merchant who offered a substantial dowry. The young married couple settled down in the city of Brod, near Yarac, where my father went into the drygoods and textile business with the help of his brothers, all successful merchants.

Unfortunately, my father, a fine man in all respects, had no head for business matters. Temperamentally he was more of a scholar than a businessman, but with an adventurous streak. Unprepared by either experience or instinct to carry on his business, he did his best to keep abreast of the considerable responsibilities and requirements of the new enterprise. It was a disaster. My father kept the business going with the help of my mother's dowry, but after two years he had to close the doors.

Somehow it happened next that my father came to be the owner of the beer and sandwich concession in a circus. In those days a circus audience consumed beer and sandwiches while watching the performance. In this way, my father found himself travelling through Europe and satisfying his adventurous spirit. Finally, he landed in Danzig, a city in East Prussia, where, shortly before the end of the century, I came into this world.

The sandwich and liquor concession was extremely profitable and required little in the way of management. Papa did well. Meanwhile, my parents received letters from Yarac imploring them to give up their vagabond life, now that they had a child who needed the stability of a permanent home. Eventually, when I was about

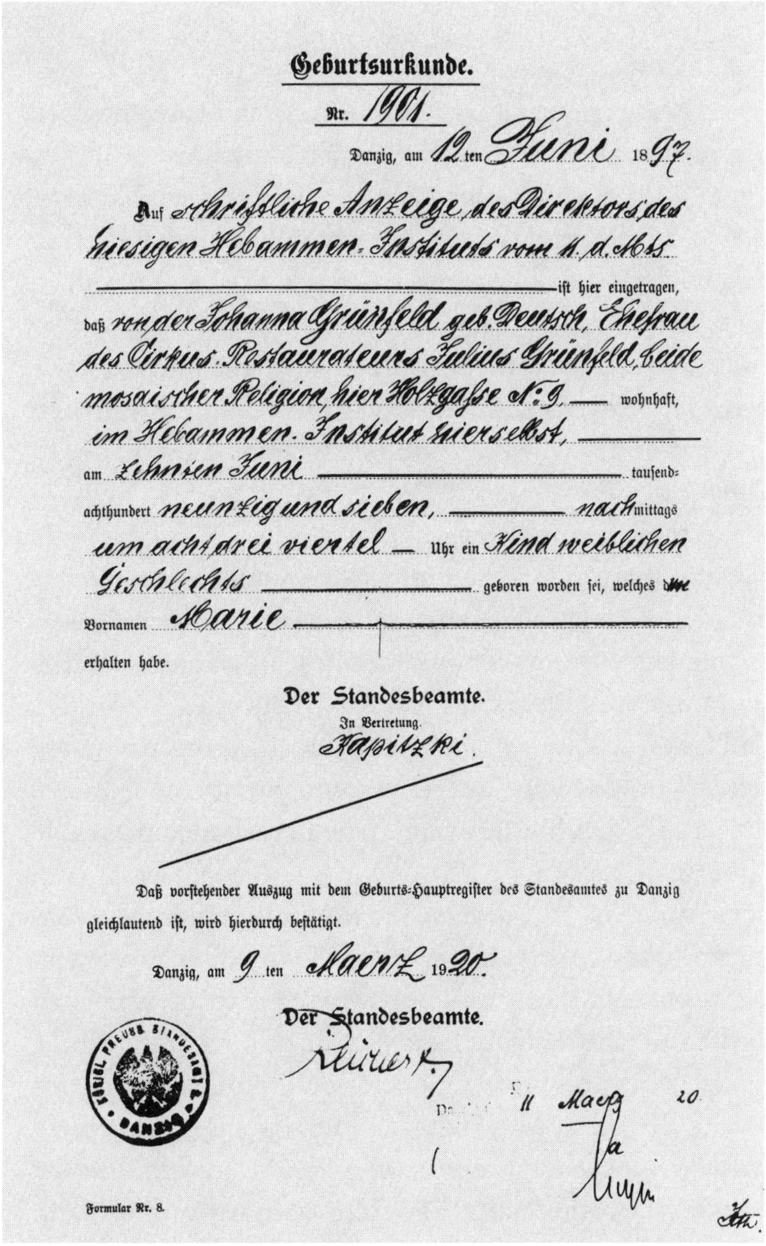

Geburtsurkunde.

Nr. *1901.*

Danzig, am *12.* ten *Juni* 18 *97.*

Auf schriftliche Anzeige des Directors des hiesigen Hebammen-Instituts vom 11. d. Mts —————————————— ist hier eingetragen,

daß *von der Johanna Grünfeld geb. Deutsch, Ehefrau des Circus-Restaurateurs Julius Grünfeld, beide mosaischer Religion, hier Holzgasse N: 9.* ——— wohnhaft, *im Hebammen-Institut hierselbst,* ————

am *Zehnten Juni* ———————————— tausend=

achthundert *neunzig und sieben,* ——— nach mittags *um acht drei viertel* — Uhr ein *Kind weiblichen Geschlechts* ——————— geboren worden sei, welches die

Vornamen *Marie* ————

erhalten habe.

Der Standesbeamte.

In Vertretung.

Kapitzki.

Daß vorstehender Auszug mit dem Geburts=Hauptregister des Standesamtes zu Danzig gleichlautend ist, wird hierdurch bestätigt.

Danzig, am *9.* ten *Maerz* 19 *20.*

Der Standesbeamte.

Reinert.

D...... 11 Maerz 20

Formular Nr. 8.

Marie Jastrow's birth certificate: "Marie, born June 10, 1897 to Johanna Grünfeld, wife of circus restauranteur Julius Grünfeld."

five, they gave up the circus business and came back to Yarac. There, my grandfather persuaded my father to open a store again, this time for general merchandise. But that enterprise did not prosper either, and my father had to close the doors once more. He was not cut out to be a merchant.

Meanwhile, word had spread of a remarkable land across the sea where a man was known to become rich and famous beyond his wildest dreams. "I am going to America," Papa said. "People have been known to make their fortunes there."

But I think my father came to America mainly for a different reason — not so much to seek his fortune, as to escape the tyranny of his family's judgment after the two business failures. In Yarac, his successful brothers and father-in-law were a constant if silent reproach. My father's need was to be free to remain poor, if that was his lot in life, without being made to feel uncomfortable about it.

He sailed in 1905, when the flow of immigrants from Europe was nearly at its peak. Every day the ocean liners brought thousands of steerage passengers, packed like cattle into the bottoms of the ships. A steerage ticket, which cost thirty dollars, only purchased a space in the cargo hold. There, hundreds of bodies were crowded together without ventilation for up to two weeks. My father said they slept on narrow shelves in compartments that reeked of old food, unwashed humanity and worse. Papa told us there was not enough water even for drinking, the food was inedible and the stench unbearable. It was not fit for animals, much less people, he said.

Then came the day when, together with his fellow passengers, my father pressed against the rail of his ocean liner as the ship approached Ellis Island. He remembered parents lifting up their children above the heads of the crowd to see the great Statue of Liberty. The immigrants stood there, crowding the rail, moist-eyed and awestruck as they viewed the Lady with her ever-burning torch of welcome.

For my father, this was what America stood for. He often said later that this was when he understood he had made the right choice, back then in 1905.

Papa's first months after he landed were heart-breaking. With his work experience consisting mainly of two failed businesses, and only a few words of English, there were no jobs to be had. Later he often told us about that time. It was the darkest period in his life. Finally, he collapsed, near starvation, on the steps of Saint Mark's Hospital on Eleventh Street. When his story came out, he had his first job in America! A mop and pail, and the title of porter. It was a complete turn-about from his former life, but suddenly it didn't matter at all. He had a place to sleep, a small income and the warm comfort of his fellow workers, who took him under their wings.

From here on, the power of my father's commitment to his new country was intense and complete. Almost immediately he acquired his first papers, which were necessary toward the final step of becoming a citizen.

The winter passed in Yarac, then another winter. Mama had never given up hope that Papa would tire of America and come back to Serbia, but his letters dimmed her hopes. "Free as a bird I am here," he wrote, "without the restrictions of Europe." The New Year of 1907 began for Papa with a better-paying job in a delicatessen on Second Avenue. Now, with the increased income, his chances were greatly improved for accumulating sufficient funds to buy cabin class tickets for Mama and me. We were not to go through the nightmare of the steerage crossing, he said. In the summer of 1907, the tickets arrived.

Mama had been dreading the day when the decision must be made to leave Yarac. On the one hand, there was the separation from her husband. On the other hand, the thought of never seeing mother, father, sister again was tearing at her heartstrings. No, she could not face that ordeal. Her husband's place was here. There was a great deal of talk, a great deal of advice, and then the final decision: Wives belonged where their husbands settled. With tearful farewells, we left Serbia, traveled to Hamburg, and crossed the ocean on the President Grant, arriving in the new world twelve days later.

Mingled hope and anxiety showed in the faces of steerage passengers crowding the decks of an immigrant ship in the early 1900s. *(opposite)*

As their ship entered New York harbor, the immigrants lined the rails to see the Statue of Liberty. Many wept.

The immigrants were still not free to enter America after they had crossed the ocean. Ellis Island officials put them through tests for mental and physical fitness, applying a nineteenth-century law that barred "idiots, insane persons, paupers, persons suffering from a loathsome or dangerous infectious disease, persons convicted of a felony...and polygamists."

opposite: Letters chalked on an immigrant's coat indicated suspected diseases. A chalked "X" meant a suspicion of feeblemindedness.

below: An immigrant fits variously shaped objects into holes on a board while the examiner times him with a stopwatch.

Doctors also looked for signs of such ailments as heart trouble, lameness, and diseases of the skin or eyes. The eye examination was somewhat painful and feared by all immigrants. Redness of the lids could mean trachoma, a highly infectious disease possibly leading to blindness. The trachoma virus was isolated later by an immigrant.

below: The examiner riveted the immigrant's gaze and used a buttonhook to turn back the eyelid in search of the telltale inflammation.

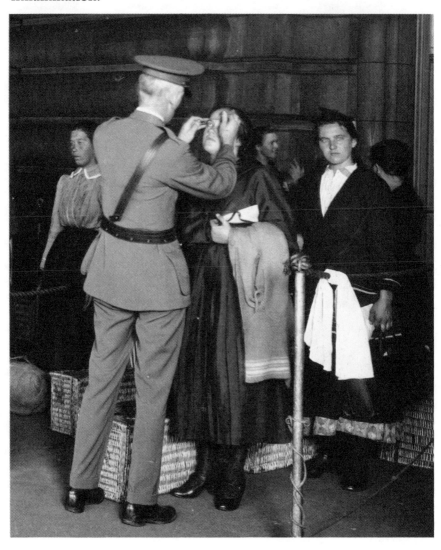

Rejected immigrants were sent back. Agonizing decisions arose for families when one member failed to pass the examinations. Should they all go back? Who should stay? Only the rejected one received free passage home; sometimes parents were separated from children because they could not afford the passage back. For good reason Ellis Island was called the "Isle of Tears."

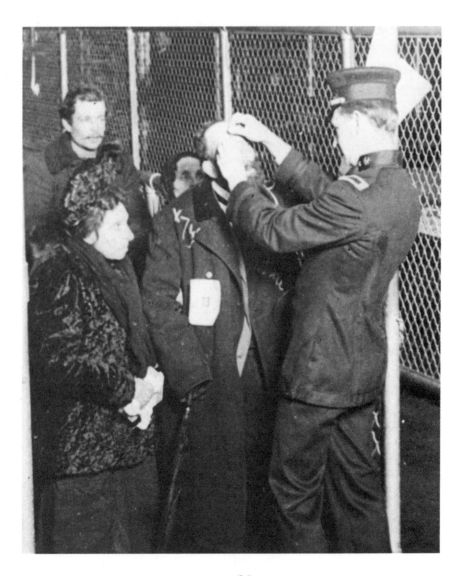

2
First Months in the New World

What a bewildering world it was. We had never seen such high buildings. Papa had prepared a two-room flat on the third floor in a five-story building on Ninth Street and Avenue C. Fearfully we ventured up those three flights on my father's solemn promise that nothing would collapse, and entered our first home in America.

Suddenly, without warning, before we had time to breathe almost, my mother threw open the window, and tore the bed apart. "My God, didn't you ever change sheets? This bed looks as if a chimney sweep has been sleeping in it." Papa looked a little startled, but soon recovered. "To tell you the truth," he said, "I waited for you — changing sheets seemed too complicated."

Mama laughed, "All this time you never —"

"Oh, yes," Papa broke in, "a neighbor, whose wife was kind enough to come in and clean once in a while. But, now that you were coming — you know, I didn't want to bother her."

Mama often talked of her first hours in America, when she and my father together cleaned the two rooms he had prepared for our arrival. "And you know what, I forgot to take my hat off and my gloves," she laughed.

In time, my mother recovered sufficiently to look America in the face. Life here was definitely not a bed of roses. Especially burdensome was the climb down three flights of stairs to the toilets. Toilets in the basement were absolutely unacceptable for my mother, even in our diminished circumstances. Since patience was not one of her virtues, she came right to the point. "I will find something better," she said.

When Papa remained silent, she added, "You can see for yourself, all those stairs down to the toilet in the cellar — no one can live this way."

The problem now was where to find a new home commensurate with our feeble resources. No one was safe from my mother's energetic inquiries about better living quarters. The weather was excellent and the neighborhood stores were crowded with people with possible information.

Well, my mother was as good as her word. "I found something better," Papa was informed that evening. "We are moving to Seventy-sixth Street." Papa's mouth dropped. "How in the world? I mean — only three weeks ago, you came off the ship. How . . .?"

"I asked people. I have a mouth. I speak. The grocery lady has a sister who lives in this place." And quickly she added, "The toilets are in the hall, not in the cellar."

No room for argument there.

"How much is the rent?" Papa asked. "Oh, nothing to worry over. Only fifty cents more," Mama answered casually, and disappeared into the kitchen. Papa went back to his paper, which he was reading sitting at the window in the other room.

What my mother had failed to add was "a week."

We moved into that Seventy-sixth Street place on a hot, muggy day in the summer of 1907. It was an improvement, but not without its thorn to prick our expectations. The toilet was in the hall on our floor, but another tenant shared hall and toilet, bringing conflicts of more than one kind. The real difficulty was that you couldn't speak about the problem. It was there all right, but of all conflicts between neighbors, this was the most difficult to tackle. All Mama said was, "Those people are impossible."

We moved again, to a flat with its own bathroom, on Ninety-second Street near First Avenue, and stayed over the winter. We were beginning to get adjusted to our new life, which was no longer so bewildering as it had seemed on that first day in Ninth Street. My parents were even growing accustomed to marvels like the horsecar and the elevated train. I do not remember horsecars in Yarac. Certainly there were no elevated trains.

The El carried my father to and from his job every day. After a while the ride on the El became a kind of social gathering. There were greetings, handclasps and laughing faces when a familiar figure boarded the train. My father loved those social train rides every morning. If this seems strange today, one must remember that New York in that immigrant period was filled with people who came from somewhere else. Alone, without family, their need was for new alliances and friendships. They needed companionship, even if only on the El.

Lifelong relationships often resulted from these rides. Sometimes friendships stemming from the El led to home invitations. There were always daughters in the house, and before you knew it there was a marriage.

The El quickly became part of our normal life, but I continued to be amazed by the sight of a carriage or a wagon going down the street without being pulled by horses. Only a few automobiles were on the street in Yorkville in 1907, but they made a strong impression on us. There were no automobiles in Yarac. At least, I never saw one.

My mother was more impressed by the clothes, especially the women's hats. Back home, a "Tuchel," or kerchief, was the headgear of most women. Only the well-to-do wore hats. Here everyone, even shopgirls, wore hats. My mother liked that. She liked the lack of class distinctions.

In June, a year after we landed, Papa heard about a brand new tenement on Eighty-first Street near York Avenue. Mama went there, saw it and was conquered. At the end of the month we moved once more. It was all there. The white porcelain sink, hot water, steam heat (no more coal to sift for the unburned ones), and, my mother's pride and joy, the private bathroom with its own toilet and a white bathtub, now located next to the bedroom off a private hall. No longer the heating of water on the stove for baths in the kitchen. After the cold-water flats, this was luxury.

And how different from Yarac, where bathrooms with toilets were nonexistent and outhouses were used, even in town. When it came to bathing, my grandfather took his morning dip in a rain barrel standing outside the kitchen door. Once a week my grandmother and the children went down to a bathhouse on the Save River, where a part of the river was cordoned off. The bathhouse had tiny cubbyholes where people changed clothes and went into the water in their nightgowns, which ballooned as they dipped up and down in the river.

As I recall, there was also no water running out of spigots in my grandfather's home. All the water was carried into the house from a well in the yard. Dishes were washed in a huge iron pot and rinsed in a second iron pot. The dishwater ran into an iron trough and then into a pipe that drained through the kitchen wall and onto the ground outside. What a blessing, what an improvement the iron sinks in our first apartments were, with their running water — even though Mama had to paint them once a week — not to forget the gleaming white porcelain sinks which she acquired in Eighty-first Street.

That modern tenement on Eighty-first Street restored my mother's confidence in the "good life" America had to offer. Our American odyssey ended; evidently Mama was convinced that from here on, "something better" was out of her reach.

My mother sighed with satisfaction, Papa with relief.

We lived in this building on East Eighty-first Street for many years, until the Great War brought changes to the street. In these years, we developed our ties to America. Here we grew roots.

The El was a social
meeting place for
the immigrants.

43

Cars were beginning to be common in New York when we arrived from Germany. By 1912, there were a million cars in America...

...but twenty million horses. Horses were still the main form of transport.

© 1910 By AMERICAN STUDIO N.Y.
WEST B'WAY N.Y. FEB. 1910 SNOW STORM.
122

47

Overworked, ema-
ciated horses were
a common sight...

49

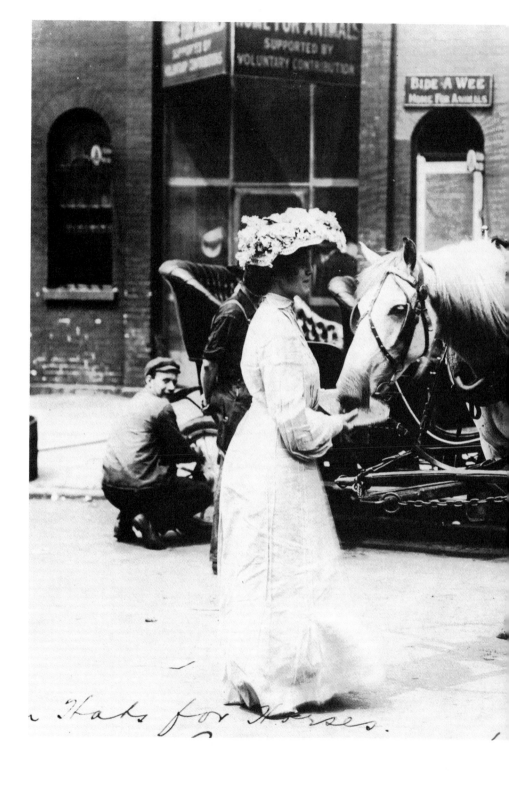

Hats for Horses.

...but this horse was well taken care of, with a sun hat courtesy of the Bide-A-Wee Home.

3
Bad Times

*I*n the winter of 1907-1908 — our first winter in New York — America experienced one of those depressions that afflicted the young country every so often. My father said they were "growing pains." This one started with a run on the Knickerbocker Bank in New York that cleaned out eight million dollars in three hours. There were other runs, and banks started holding onto their cash and calling in loans. Businesses could not meet their obligations, and people lost their jobs.

We immigrants did not know anything about this. All we knew was that neighbors were working half shifts or nothing. Bad times, they called it. For a time my father's delicatessen job held fast, but with the additional rent of two dollars a month in our latest home on Eighty-first Street, Mama had all she could do to make ends meet.

Suddenly Papa found his life turned upside down. The delicatessen where he worked had its own "bad time". Papa was out of a job. They presented him with a salami and wished him luck.

By this time some of our neighbors had been out of work for weeks. It was then that Papa came home with stories of furniture piled in front of buildings. "I tell you," he exploded, "it's a heartbreaking thing to see people sitting on their belongings, empty-eyed and without hope."

Mama said, "My God! Is such a thing possible? To throw people out of their homes when there is no job!"

"Well, it is terrible. But maybe the landlord has his own problems, if the rent money doesn't come in."

"I think, it could be, we will be next. We owe two months already —"

"Never — In Resch's house nobody —"

In this respect we were lucky. Mr. Resch, our landlord, who owned two buildings in the street, never evicted anyone. There were always extenuating circumstances to be considered, he said. Rent available or not, no tenants were evicted from their homes in his buildings. When better days came and jobs were found, he expected people to meet their obligations. If pockets were empty, he waited for better times.

Papa joined the ranks of the unemployed. Day by day, there were bitter experiences and disappointments. "I will take anything," he said, "even if I have to clean houses."

Well, my father did not do house cleaning. He accepted work in a small family hotel in the Bath Beach section of Brooklyn, New York. There was one drawback. It was a sleep-in job. Twenty dollars a month and one free afternoon every two weeks came with it.

"But what will you do there?" Mama wanted to know. "I mean, why do they need you to work in the night?"

"I have no idea how they plan their hotel," Papa answered, "But I do know that something better will come along. In the meantime, twenty dollars will keep you in food. The rent I have arranged with Mr. Resch. When we have it, we will pay."

"And he agreed?"

"What can I say? There is heart — yes, he agreed."

Papa packed his suitcase, promised to be home on his free afternoon, and off he went, leaving my mother to face the new world of America alone. Mama and I stood at the door, staring after his retreating figure, going slowly down the stairs.

There was not much my mother could do; conditions were critical. It was only a short time since we had moved into that modern Eighty-first Street tenement with the white porcelain sink, steam heat, and horrendous rent of nine dollars a month.

This was what my mother dreaded the most — to face the new world of America alone. A terrible attack of homesickness overcame her, triggered by my father's absence. She was stricken by a sense of loss; she said she felt abandoned. There were no crying spells, but Mama would read and re-read the letters from "home".

Of course my father had no knowledge of the overwhelming loneliness his absence caused. I was sworn to secrecy.

Two weeks later when Papa came home on his free afternoon, I kept my silence. And then he kissed us again with, "On my free day I will be home," and Mama watched him again pack some clean linens in a bag. Surely, I thought, she would object; but Papa was gone.

The next day my mother tore the house apart. Never was there such a frenzy of cleaning. Then she sat down at the table, my mother who was not given to tears, put her head down on her arms and remained there uncontrollably sobbing, with me watching and feeling as useless as only a ten-year-old can. Suddenly she sat up abruptly, listening as if something had shocked her. I followed my mother's eyes to the door. A key grated in its lock — Papa walked in, and Mama almost fainted.

"What is it then? Why are you home?" Then louder, "WHY ARE YOU HOME?" My mother, never known for great restraint, gave her voice its full volume.

"Calm yourself, Um Himmelswillen!"

"All right, but why are you home? What happened?"

"Nothing happened — I mean, nothing — sit down,

already — I have good news." My father then sat down at the table opposite Mama. "I have a job," he said simply. Before he could say more, Mama screamed, "How? My God! A job? With money every week —?"

"Seven dollars a week — and yes, I will stay home."

"But how —?"

Papa went into the story of the guest at the hotel. "He found that I could speak German. A job was open as porter in this import and export house — Bawo and Dotter. He asked why I came to this country. I decided to tell the truth, that I was not much of a businessman; I lost your dowry, I told him. He liked that."

Papa kept his job with Bawo and Dotter for many years, until America entered the war in 1917 and they were forced to close their doors. The import and export business was one of the casualties of the war with Germany.

Papa started with Bawo and Dotter at eight dollars a week, about four hundred dollars a year. His salary went up after it came to the firm's attention that he could read and write German as well as speak it. Papa was transferred to the shipping department. He packed the very fine china and scientific glassware, and handled the German bills of lading.

Of course, these wages would not be enough to live on today, but as I remember it, they were sufficient to cover expenses then, with milk four cents a quart, eggs ten cents a dozen, and chickens sixteen cents a pound; and a lung, including the heart, for a few cents and more often than not free with the purchase of meat. That lung made a delicious meal. My mother cut up the lung and heart, browned onions in chicken fat and covered the meat with the onions. She added a cup of chicken soup, salt and plenty of paprika from Paprika Weiss to give a nice reddish-brown color. With rice or noodles on the side, lung goulash was a tasty, protein-rich food and only cost a few cents.

This way of surviving the newcomers soon learned. There was never enough money, but Mama managed with what she had. Poor, we never felt; it was just that we had empty pockets.

The Panic of 1907 started with a run on the Knickerbocker Trust Company on Fifth Avenue...

...and spread to the smaller banks in which poorer people and immigrants had their savings.

KERS | TELEGRAPH & CABLE OFFICE

61

Evictions were
common. A
family's
possessions were
piled up on the
street.

63

In good times wages were seven or eight dollars a week but prices were low. A meal could be bought for pennies...

...and made-to-measure skirts were seventy-five cents.

4
Making Do

*A*s far as I remember, every apartment had a large double tub in the kitchen in those days. Mondays were normally set as washdays. My mother started the day in her washday outfit, whose absurdity reflected her opinion of that hated weekly chore. Mama would wrap her head in a turban-like cover made of several pieces of worn toweling held together with a few safety pins. Next she would put on an old sheet into which she had cut a hole for her head, and then fasten the sheet around her with a huge safety pin. A pair of rubber boots encased bare feet "in case water runs over". It never did.

The wash was done in the kitchen. First my mother boiled the soiled things in a huge kettle into which she would slice a bar of yellow Octagon soap, as well as a good portion of sal-soda. She said the boiling and the soda did the work. After the steaming wash was transferred to the tub, Mama went to work on it with the bathroom plunger, which replaced the traditional washboard in our house. Her reasoning was simply that if clogged pipes were cleared with the plunger, it could draw out the soiled deposits that had been brought to the surface with the boiling. She already had the plunger. Why spend money on a washboard? The plunger seems to have worked. Washboards never appeared in my mother's kitchen. That was fifty cents saved — half a day's work for Papa.

My mother always patched, covered, manipulated, and made do with what she had on hand. I have always felt wonderment at the way she managed on Papa's salary, which was about eight dollars a week. In New York, in those early days, most households had an icebox. In our house, Mama found a way to make a washtub take the place of the icebox.

Mama put a twenty-five-pound block of ice in the tub and covered it with moist newspaper, the idea being to freeze the paper. The block of ice cost ten cents. Then a large corrugated box was inverted over the ice. Under that inverted box went all our perishables. Items like butter were placed directly on top of the paper-covered ice; milk and other items went next to it. On top of the box and around the side, my mother wrapped more wet newspaper. She believed in wet paper. That kept everything fresh. Of course, we never tried to keep uncooked food. Meat was cooked the day it was bought; milk, which was unpasteurized, was boiled immediately. The ice lasted three or four days — three cents a day for refrigeration.

We never bought ice in the winter — that meant twenty cents saved every week. The window box, attached to the ledge outside the window in the winter months, replaced the iceman. "Why pay for ice when the winter freeze provides it free," Mama said, adding, "And thank God for boxes with a shelf." These were orange crates provided by the grocer. A partition down the middle of the crate made two food compartments. And it worked. Of course, there was the disadvantage of the cold blasts blowing into the kitchen whenever that outdoor icebox was used. A heavy shawl, hanging on a hook beside the window, solved the problem for Mama. For us, who felt the chilly blast in the rest of the apartment, Mama said, "I will close the door —"

"But," we said, "there is no door."

"Resch will put a door in," — every room needs a door, I will tell him." Eventually the bedroom door was used in the kitchen. A sheet, which Mama dyed brown, served as a portier between the bedroom and the front room.

The window box worked surprisingly well. Winters were longer and colder in those days, and there was never any spoilage. Surprisingly, too, the space inside the window box seemed to expand with every extra container of food that needed cooling. All the years, into the twenties, window boxes could be seen outside kitchen windows in our part of Yorkville.

Then, one day, we had a proper icebox. My father had decided to build an icebox to put all other iceboxes to shame. The store-bought iceboxes were too much money, he said. Besides, they did not keep the ice from melting before its time.

Papa set to work and put together a fine, sturdily built icebox. Except that he placed the insulated chamber at the bottom of the box, instead of the top where everyone else put it. Papa had the idea for this "improvement" because heat rises, he said, and the rising heat melts the ice on the top too fast. So — the ice chamber was placed below.

Mama was delighted with her new icebox. Alas! She soon discovered that, sturdily built and all, the box barely kept the food cool. Something was wrong. But what?

Mama did a bit of sleuthing. She learned that the ice chamber belongs on top for the very reason that Papa had put it on the bottom — because cold stays below and will not travel upward sufficiently to cool things. Papa was right; heat rises. The ice on the bottom didn't melt, but the food spoiled.

Now there was a problem: how to get my father to accept this new development. My mother went directly to the point. "I think — and don't be angry — but I think the ice has to be on top." She added, "I went to Rosenberg's. He told me. He gave me some technical reason, I can't remember."

Surprisingly, Papa did not become angry. With a laugh he said, "I will fix it." Whereupon, he simply turned the box upside down. The controversial ice chamber was now on top where it belonged. Legs were detached and brought down, a new method for drainage was devised. The upside-down icebox worked very well.

My mother used it for quite a few years. Early in the twenties that marvel, the frigidaire, entered her kitchen. But to my father's great delight, Mama never considered that upside-down icebox as anything but her special possession. She kept odds and ends in it for years until my father died. After that we did not see it in its usual place.

It was never discussed.

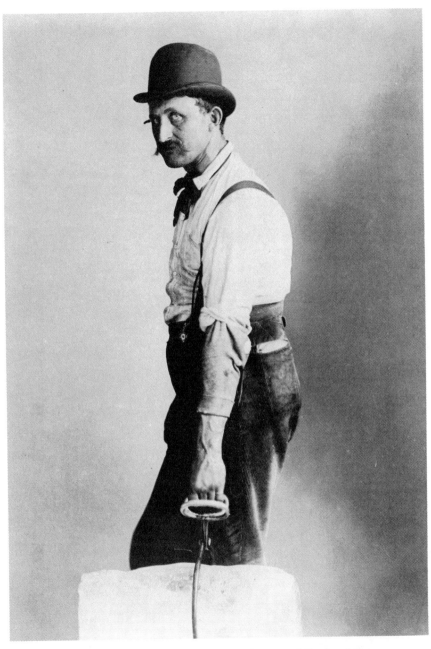

Twice a week the iceman carried a new block of ice up the stairs.

Clothes and sheets were wrung out by hand and dried on lines strung from the kitchen window to a pole twenty-five feet away. If they dripped down on the wash from lower floors, there were loud complaints from the neighbors below.

Sometimes a line slipped off a pulley.

For that, linemen went through the street with coils of rope slung over their shoulders, calling "Lineman! Fix your line!" A new line cost two dollars, which was two days' pay.

73

5
The Flatiron Building

One day, when we had not been in America very long, Papa took me by the hand. "Today we will walk to Twenty-third Street, where we will see something you never could imagine, not in your wildest dreams — we will see the Flatiron Building, a world wonder."

Mama said, "Is it far to walk to this Twenty-third Street?"

"Not far, not more than a mile, I think. And we can take the streetcar if you think it will be too much for the child."

"I can walk, Papa. I can walk," I said.

"Good! Good!" Papa said. Then turning to my mother, he cried, "I tell you, never before has there been a time when a country has put up such a structure as the Flatiron Building."

And with my father's hand in mine we set out that Monday on the first of many sightseeing adventures. On the way, Papa did his best to translate the words "Flatiron Building" into German. Mama repeated with Papa, "Flatiron Building," several times. Two words of English she achieved that day, as we marched to Twenty-third Street. And there, at Twenty-third Street in the triangle of Broadway and Fifth Avenue, stood Papa's wonder: an amazing structure reaching into the sky, with many windows reflecting tiny golden flecks of sunlight. We craned our necks and gazed up in awe. For us, who had never come in contact with buildings higher than two stories until we came to our first five-story tenement in America, this brick edifice, with row upon row of windows reaching into the sky, seemed nothing short of fantastic.

"My God!" Mama cried. "How do they keep it from falling down? What in Heaven's name holds it up?"

Papa answered, "It's built on a steel frame — the whole building. And that is the wonder of it, I think."

"Papa," I asked, "How does a person come down from the top?"

Papa laughed. "First you must go up, Liebchen, to come down."

"But this is terrible!" Mama exclaimed. "So many steps to climb — do people live in this Flatiron Building?"

"No, my father said, "but people come here to work. And there are machines that lift you up and down. People ride up and down in these elevators all day. No one walks."

Mama's eyes opened wide. "You mean, like the elevated that takes you every place in the city?"

"Well, something like it — only it goes up and down, instead of back and forth." Papa said. "We will go up."

My mother had her doubts about a machine that could fall down if whatever holds it up were to break.

"Maybe some other time," she said. "When we have more experience in such things."

But Papa insisted. We stepped into the elevator with me clinging to his arm. My mother frowned but followed. The machine started, and no sooner was there an upward movement than my stomach fell, turned some somersaults, and emptied on the floor. Mama defended me. She said her stomach did not feel "so good either."

Papa cleaned the mess with a newspaper the uniformed attendant furnished. And I thought I would die of shame.

"This way of going up and down is not in God's order, I think," said Mama. "It is possible to break one's back, if a person is not experienced. Certainly one should not eat before putting foot into an elevator."

My father looked properly lectured. "I'm sorry. I did not mean to cause so much trouble. But, in America, that's the way things are. Machines run everything."

After that little calamity that befell me, we got out of the elevator and trudged up the stairs, stopping on each floor to view the city below us, talking to people, enjoying every minute of it, until Papa took his watch in hand. "Four already —," Mama said, "My God! How the time does fly." And Papa said, "We will go down and then walk east to Second Avenue. There we will go south." We left the building and started to walk home. After a while, Papa carried me. Taking the trolley was out of the question.

Mama would never have considered taking the trolley, with the expense of the fare nagging at her frugal mind. Never would she have been comfortable riding in luxury when walking would get her home just as well. She would have brooded over the many necessities the fare could have purchased. I have memories of my mother agonizing over a ten cent purchase. Could she have done better? Might she have done without? And saved it for a "rainy day"? Mama's rainy days were always clouded with second thoughts and misgivings.

When we reached Second Avenue, we turned down toward Ninth Street. Walking home, Papa suddenly suggested the automat. "Let us make it a holiday with a good ending. For five cents we can get a pot of baked beans, and —"

"No," Mama interrupted. "I have a chicken soup ready. We will go home. Nothing better than a good, hot plate of chicken soup for the fatigued body."

"A good, hot plate of chicken soup" — in our house,

the alpha and omega. How often have I heard my mother say, "I will make a chicken soup today. It will make you feel better." A cold, an aching muscle, a bruised elbow — Mama would expound the theory of that steaming-hot, aromatic, impossible-to-describe remedy for all problems in our house.

There could be no warmer welcome for a husband, coming home from a ten-hour work day, than a whiff of steaming chicken soup, or stew, or baking bread, to get the gastric juices ready for their job.

I can see my father, with an expectant smile: "Ah! That smells like paprikasch." Chicken — browned, with onions added, slowly cooked in tomato sauce or, as mother did it, with crushed fresh tomatoes. For seasoning, add enough hot, red paprika to make the eyes water with the first bite. At least that is the way Papa liked it. Served on a bed of broad noodles. Sour cream could be added before serving. Though we did not keep a kosher kitchen, Mama preferred it without sour cream.

Upon coming home from his day's work, Papa would sniff the air, make his remark "That smells like — (the supper of the day)," wash his hands, and sit down at the table. His day's work done, his face would light up when Mama came into the dining-room (which was also the front room) with the steaming, aromatic platter of the evening meal. This must have been, for my father and mother, the moment of perfect understanding.

The Flatiron Building was an American wonder in the early 1900s—one of the first buildings in which the weight of the floors was carried by a steel skeleton. The walls were hung on the steel framework like curtains to keep out the weather.

The Flatiron Building filled a triangle between Fifth Avenue and Broadway at Twenty-third Street. Ankle watchers at the windy Twenty-third Street intersection were shooed away by the police—hence the expression "23 skidoo."

6
How Rich is Rich?

*M*y father was an inveterate sight-seer. His free days were spent on little adventures, touring the city. After dinner, on Monday, his day off, Papa would suggest, "Today we will see —" and he would name the tour in his mind. An architecturally unique building, museums — we went through the Metropolitan Museum more often than I can count. I loved it. My mother did not always accompany us; her interest in America was more practical. My father saw his new country in a more imaginative, adventurous light. And he had a story for everything.

One day he said, "Today we will walk to the Wana-maker Building," and he recited the tale of the Philadelphia merchant, John Wanamaker, while walking to that building. John Wanamaker, Papa said, early in his life took over the A. T. Stewart and Company store on Astor Place and Ninth Street. Whereupon he made great changes, including the name. Wanamaker's was destined to be one of the best known department stores in New York City.

"And when you grow up you will be rich enough to shop in this fine establishment," Papa said.

"How rich will I have to be?" I wanted to know.

"When you have enough money to pay for the things that store carries."

It became quite a challenge, this having sufficient money for Wanamaker's. Several years later, when we had already moved into that modern tenement in Eighty-first Street, I achieved the impossible. I was neither grown up nor rich, but I did shop in Wana-maker's store.

Early in our immigrant days my father had become involved with contests offered periodically by the *Staats-Zeitung* — the German–language newspaper — with prizes for the fortunate winners.

There were word contests, picture contests, contests about musicians and artists and their works. Papa entered them all, hopefully, with my mother wondering why, since no prize ever came his way.

"Everything comes to him who waits," Papa would say.

"But how many years will you spend money on stamps and extra paper, waiting?" When Papa remained silent, my mother went back into the kitchen. A hopeless addiction. She sighed, resigned.

Well, my father waited. "Everything comes to him who waits." And one winter day Lady Luck remembered my father, who had entered a contest involving artists and paintings. I can still see Papa's face when he opened an evelope expecting the usual thank-you note, and instead saw bouncing out a certificate for third prize. "I won! I won!" "MY GOD, I WON!" he cried. It was a twenty-five dollar certificate involving, of all stores, Wanamaker's.

Here we were, with twenty-five dollars to buy our heart's desire in that high-class store where, as Papa said, only rich people shopped.

And I wondered how rich was twenty-five dollars. At that time in my life the economics of twenty-five dollars was rather hazy. So I asked, "Papa, how much is twenty-five dollars?"

"Twenty-five dollars is three weeks' pay," Mama answered for my father. "It is a great deal of money. If we could put it in the bank, the certificate, that is where it would rest, but —"

"But God, in His wisdom has decreed it otherwise," Papa said, interrupting. "We will go to Wanamaker's and have a wonderful time spending twenty-five dollars without considering —" and here Papa looked at my mother — "getting the better of the bargain."

"Oh you! What do you want of me? It is not easy —"

"I know, I know," Papa laughed. "I was only teasing."

"Well, some husband you are, spending money like a drunkard," Mama said heatedly. "And furthermore, we will decide what to buy here, in our kitchen, where it will be easy to remember that our pockets are not filled with gold."

Papa put down his cup of coffee. "What are you saying? With this gift we will shop like people who are used to shopping. Today you will not "handel". Today you will select, ask how much, and I will pay."

Mama shook her head slowly. "Has this money gone to your head?"

"Maybe," laughed Papa. "And it would be nice to see you enjoying it too. I never realized how wonderful it is, the thrill of buying without feeling guilty."

And Mama said, "But — I mean — maybe the merchandise there, in that fine store, is very expensive, maybe, not for people like us?"

"What people? In America everybody is the same," Papa cried. He took his watch out of his vest pocket. "It is ten already. Before you know it, the day will be gone. Put your hat on — and to please me, let this be a holiday — and no handeling."

How I remember that afternoon. We arrived home loaded with packages. Mama had a new coat, soft and woolly; Papa was the proud owner of a new Sunday suit; for me Mama remembered several school costumes

— pleated skirts and middy blouses, and black stockings with high-button shoes, which required a button hook. Mama's shoes were high-button, always.

I can still see, in my mind's eye, the delight in my father's face as he signed for the purchases for which the certificate was paying. These uninhibited selections, "without feeling guilty," were a great delight.

That evening, while we were eating, Mama suddenly said, "All I know is that in Wanamaker's customers throw their money out, or they might as well, for the way they buy things."

"Now, again, you are not satisfied — so much we acquired for my prize certificate — what more do you want?"

"It is only" — Mama said unhappily. "Well, to tell you the truth, for me shopping is no pleasure if I have to pay what is asked right away. I would rather shop at Rosenberg's."

And I believe she would have. She missed the challenge of matching wits with Mr. Rosenberg and the resulting pleasure in the prize she carried home.

Rosenberg's, on First Avenue and Eighty-fourth Street, was the poor man's department store. With my father's earnings as low as they were in the first few years, Mama could not have solved her budget problems without bargain purchases at Rosenberg's. The dented pot, the faded blouse that could be rejuvenated with RIT, or the bargain "just for you," which, more often than not, Mama would bring triumphantly home.

"Oh," Papa laughed, "Now I see, you missed "handeling" maybe?"

"Well, some husband you are," Mama said heatedly. "Not one word did you allow me say, when I could see that the blouse we bought could be much cheaper. They would have reduced the —"

Papa was shocked. "You are not serious? In Wanamaker's no one reduces."

"Well, for this reason, no one is happy shopping there. Did you see one happy face, I ask you? Silent like a tomb it was there."

"Why people who buy in Wanamaker's store are not happy, was not our business to consider. And we did buy many —"

"But we paid too much for everything," insisted my mother.

Thereafter, Papa entered many contests. Occasionally, there were some minor responses, but never again a winning prize. And then, suddenly, it ended. And I have to say here, to my mother's great relief. The way she looked at it, Lady Luck had favored us once, and beautifully; there would not be a second time. She knew these things. She was fearful of retribution, if we showed ourselves greedy.

"Anyway," she said, "I would have enjoyed myself better, shopping in Rosenberg's."

Only rich people shopped at Wanamakers—the large building in the background of this 1905 photograph.

7
Growing Into It

Our mothers had to be skill-
ful shoppers. I remember how my mother found a coat
for me at a bargain price. One evening Papa was
reading his newspaper. My mother, opposite him, with
darning needle in hand, looked up.

"I have something to say — put the paper down for a
minute." Papa took his eyes from his favorite column.

"Do you think we could get a coat for the child this
winter?" she said.

"Well, we are a little short — what is wrong with her
winter coat?" Papa asked. "Nothing," Mama laughed,

"Only she has gotten bigger, but the coat refused to keep up with her."

"Yes, I noticed. Our little girl is growing into quite a young lady. She is — I can't keep up with it — she is ten?"

"Eleven," Mama said, "And she really needs a coat."

"Of course, if you can manage —" "Well, Mama broke in hastily, "I thought we would pay only half of everything — if they get something they'll be satisfied."

"Whom do you have in mind," Papa wanted to know.

"I was thinking — and don't get angry, but I think maybe we'll begin with the rent —"

"No! Cut corners, but not with the rent money."

"Well, all right, but — can we borrow ten dollars from the Lodge? I have to get my shoes —"

Papa's lodge was the Turnverein, on East Eighty-second Street off Lexington Avenue. It is still there, although the German-American community that supported it has largely moved away to New Jersey and Long Island. In Papa's time it was a beehive of activity with singing classes, ballet classes, classes in German literature.

Papa reflected on the possibility of borrowing from the Lodge. Borrowing from the Turnverein was something to be done once or twice in your lifetime, for true emergencies.

"I really hate to — yet, it will be the way, I suppose, to get that coat." After a pause Papa asked, "Where will you go, to Rosenberg's?"

"That would be wonderful, only Rosenberg's don't carry coats. I have heard of a place downtown, Division Street. The streetcar will take us."

"Division Street? That doesn't sound too reliable."

"People in this house buy there — a good place to get bargains, they told me."

"Well, go with God's help."

Arriving in Division Street, Mama focused on the store fronts, paying no attention — at least pretending not to notice the merchants hawking their wares.

"Lady, come in — we have for you the most exquisite suit, fresh from Fifth Avenue — the price — unbelievable — then, noticing my arms sticking half out of my sleeves — he came toward me. "This young lady — what a beauty, may she live to be a hundred — have I a coat for her, only millionaires have the luck to wear. Come in — see for yourself, the bargains."

It was a tug-of-war between us and the very determined storekeeper. He won, we were in. Mama followed him to the rear of the store. It was a gloomy interior, illuminated with a light not worthy of its name.

"I would like a brown or a green, but brown I like better," Mama said. The man brought a brown coat. "What a perfect fit," he cried. Mama said, "It's too small." The man looked pained. "But the bigger one, she will swim in it."

"No," Mama said. "She will grow into it." The man brought a bigger coat. Mama said, "The brown is too dark. She is only a little girl. Such a color is for old ladies. Thank you —" And she turned to go out, pulling me with her.

The shopkeeper glared, turned, and out the door he went to snare another customer. Mama had become persona non grata.

Mama did buy a coat for me that day, oversized for "growing into," but of a mud color impossible to describe. The coat had passed for a pleasing brown in the dim light of the shop's interior. When we arrived home, Mama was in shock. As soon as she recovered, the coat traveled back to Division Street. The man never heard of us. Finally, after my mother's voice rose loud enough to be heard in City Hall, his memory magically returned. Then came some haggling. A reduction was agreed upon and, happily, Mama decided that the color was not so bad after all.

I smile as I see myself, in my mind's eye, trudging to school, battling the wind with my oversized coat flopping about. The color was the least of my problems. Mama had little to offer in the alteration department. Sleeves were tucked under and pinned at a few points. The true measure of her loving but unskilled needlework was the hem of my winter coat. She did her best but her hems were of uncertain length. She never measured and she never cut. She just basted, because every year you grew, and the hem had to come down. Finally, when you grew into it, the coat was worn out. Children in our neighborhood never had a coat that fit.

There was a "growing into" for shoes as well. As is

generally known, children have a way of out-growing shoes more often than science can explain or the average family budget can provide for. For that problem, our parents had newspapers to stuff into toes of shoes several sizes too big. The problem, here, was that unlike coats, shoes had soles which made contact with cement streets, bringing additional expense at the corner shoe-maker's. Often, as Mama bemoaned this problem, she cried, "Again you have a hole in your shoe!" Where-upon she would take a cardboard, cut it to size and fit it inside the troublesome shoe. "And don't walk so hard on the sidewalk, you hear?"

Hand-me-downs, from child to child, were a matter of course. Exchanges with neighbors were not uncom-mon. In our block, an exchange was considered "I got a new coat." Somebody else's coat, purchased or ex-changed, became your "new coat". I'm certain that many children, in those early immigrant times, never knew there were merchants who supplied wearing ap-parel in shops.

That is the way it was when I was growing up. Mothers were mistresses of all trades. They altered as best they could. How they must have dreaded it, the mothers without skills. But we children never noticed. What our mothers did seemed perfect to us. It never oc-curred to us to feel the lack of anything our parents could not afford. Weekly allowances were unheard of. Family life was built on warm devotion to children by parents, and an unquestioning acceptance of parental actions by children. Children understood the endless days of trial and anxiety that were the parent's lot.

Were we better off? Is today's child better off?

Buying a coat on
the Lower East
Side.

8
Study Anyway!

*M*y parents probably never quite realized the most important advantage the new country offered its newcomers until it confronted them when they settled in their Eighty-first Street home. That building diagonally across, on the corner, was no ordinary structure. It was in fact a school building, P.S. 96.

I am certain that few immigrants had any idea, before they came here, of that wonder of America, the public school system.

Never was there such an awakening in people of the desire for learning. The concern of parents for the education of the children was the most important element in their lives. It became a part of a belief in existing for the future, and never mind the present. Parents thought of only one thing, that their children would go to school, learn, and have a better life than they had.

Few parents did not plan on City College for their children, at least for their sons. They were never in doubt about that. All dreams and hopes drew their inspiration from the promise of the free educational system. "Study hard and some day you will be, maybe, a landlord like Mr. Resch" — Mr. Resch was the owner of our building, the captain of our precinct, and the classic success story in our neighborhood, "Arrived from the old country only twenty years before, and look at him now. In this country you can be anything you wish."

"Study hard." No matter if a child had musical talent. "A musician? My God! What kind of living is that? You want to spend your life playing in back yards, for people to throw pennies down for you to pick up?"

As an incentive to rise above such a station in life, parents pointed out their own uneducated fate, promising a future full of rich rewards "if you study hard and learn how to become a success."

Being a success meant anything that had to do with books. Study hard and opportunities will open to be anything you wish — a teacher, maybe even a doctor, or captain of the district. "Look at Mr. Resch."

As the children of newcomers, we understood well the uncertainties of the immigrant status. As a result, before anything else, we set to work to learn the new language. Actually, we had no choice. Teachers in my time had no qualms about deflating egos and were unconcerned about enhancing our "inner resources." They taught us relentlessly and thoroughly. Each teacher had forty of us in a class to contend with. Sensibilities were not coddled. There was no time for special attention to slow learners. It was learn with the rest or stay behind.

Came an unsatisfactory report: "For this I crossed the ocean in steerage, so my son should be a nothing, a nobody?" "Take your books and study." "What, no homework? Study anyway! So you'll know what the teacher asks you tomorrow."

"But Pa, I don't know what to study, with no homework."

"Study everything. You got plenty of books."

"Pa, I had a hundred today in arithmetic."

"So, you want a medal? For doing what you gotta do anyway?"

"Tomorrow is Saturday, Pa, can I study tomorrow, please?"

"Study today. Never put off till tomorrow . . ." Slap!

"Pa, you hurt my ear."

"Good — maybe this will teach you not to put off — put a warm towel on — and some day you will thank me."

Our parents believed that anything which hurt us for our own good would be rewarded in a future accounting of our virtues.

A note from the teacher created shock waves in the home as well as embarrassment for parents who had never quite mastered the language in America.

"What for you bring this note? You did something?"

"I only —" "So you were bad in school!"

In many cases the child had to read his own obituary. "The teacher wants you to come to school to see the principal."

"What for should I go to school to see your teacher?"

"I — I," the kid stammers.

"So, you don't remember?" — the usual knuckles-rap on the head. "Maybe now you will know what you did."

"I didn't do nothing, Ma. I only had to pick up a pencil from the floor."

"Maybe the teacher saw something you did when you picked up the pencil?"

"I pulled Sophy's hair — she always sticks out her tongue at me, Mama."

The mother's lips twitch. "So, all right — don't pull hair no more. Don't sit behind Sophy no more. Tell the teacher I said she should move you or her."

"Yes, Mama. But you should better write her a note!"

"All right, you write — I'll make my cross."

Our parents had great admiration for teachers. This attitude was so general that anything accomplished in the classroom was considered the highest of all achievements. And the teacher, who ruled in that dedicated place of learning, had the highest rank in parental esteem.

If, by any chance, a mother met her child's teacher on the street she would become unsettled, and wipe her hand on her apron before extending it. Often she would dip into a kind of slight curtsey and consider the meeting the most momentous event in her life. Unfortunately, the language difficulty often formed a barrier to any extended conversation. And the teachers, always beautifully dressed in long skirts and high collars, were held in awe by those simple immigrant mothers, who saw them as living in another world.

No parent would presume to question the decision of a teacher who had punished a culprit for some infraction by keeping him after school. Often the child would be subjected to parental discipline as well.

"What for did the teacher keep you in?"

"I didn't do nothing, Ma."

"Maybe to keep her company, there in the school, she kept you in."

There was silence. "Or maybe I should say something to Papa?"

"No Ma, don't tell Papa. I'll never do it again, never."

"All right, now you remembered what you did, so tell me."

"I didn't do my homework. The teacher made me do it in school, after everybody went home."

"Oh, so what did you do on the table yesterday if not your homework?" Silence, "You did something — what?" A knuckles-rap on the head.

"I was drawing a picture."

"A picture you were drawing? What for?"

"I like to put pictures on paper."

There was stunned silence. "Well, all right. But don't make no more pictures instead of homework. You hear!"

"Ma, I won't make no more pictures instead of homework."

"All right. This time I won't tell Papa. But no more pictures."

No parent, when I was growing up, felt obliged to explain to a child the reason for his punishment. It was enough that there had been a transgression. Our parents laid down the rules and we children were expected to obey. For children who disobeyed, the fastest, most effective route toward good behavior was taken with whatever was within reach of a mother's hand. A spoon, when bounced off heads, brought positive reform. You knew immediately what was expected of you. Today's advice on child-rearing had little meaning for parents who were struggling to gain a foothold in the new country.

I know that among us children there was no animosity toward parents, perhaps because there was no confusion about who we were and what the purpose of our life was. The need was to survive. Parents and children — each had his role, and each lived within it. We did not know that fathers were supposed to be pals. Nor were mothers supposed to be like sisters. They were plain mother and father, who worked hard to rear us.

Immigrant children took school seriously.

We pledged alle-
giance to the flag
every morning.

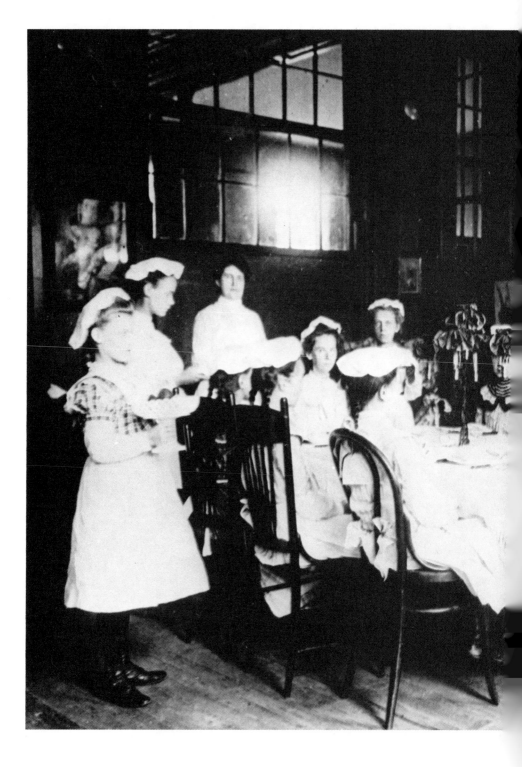

Domestic science classes were an important part of the curriculum.

9
Every Family Had a Boarder

No one we knew ever ate in a restaurant. Bachelors took a room with a family. Everybody had a boarder "to help pay expenses." Room rent was a dollar fifty to two dollars a month. With eight-dollars-a-week wages, the extra money was essential. Usually the boarder ate with the family. Weekday meals were twenty-five to thirty-five cents. Sunday dinners were more.

We took a boarder in Eighty-first Street after we were there a little more than a year. His parents and my mother's parents were neighbors in Yarac. The children took lessons together from a traveling tutor who came once a week, going from family to family and town to town. That was the extent of my mother's formal education. I do not recall there being public schools in Serbia. Certainly not in Yarac.

I do not remember the name of the newcomer, but I will call him Stepan. That was a common name in Serbia. Stepan rang our bell one day. My mother looked — "It's me, Stepan." Then in sudden recognition she turned pale. "Stepan! My God! It is really you?" Mama laughed, then she began to cry. "I can't believe it," Mama said. "But come in — don't stand in the door. I can't believe it. Someone from home. I can't believe it," Mama kept saying.

Soon our neighbors heard the good news. A friend from the old country had arrived in our house. They came to greet Stepan and to congratulate the family. Our rooms were filled with people. Mama put on the coffeepot, cut the Streussel Kuchen into serving sizes, filled a plate with thin bread-and-butter slices, and presided over her guests. When Papa came home from work in the evening, the party broke up. Seven o'clock — their own menfolk were probably home, too. Hands were shaken — all wished the newcomer good luck.

When Stepan saw my father he came out of the front room. Papa seemed stunned. "Stepan, you, here in America?" The two clasped hands. "Gruss Gott, Herr Grunfeld." While Mama saw the last of her guests to the door, the two men were already toasting eternal friendship over glasses of Slivowitz, which my father had hoarded all this time for appropriate occasions. Glasses clicked, "To your welcome!" Again, "Your health!" "To America," Papa said, "You must stay with us until you get settled." He remembered the anguish of his first lonely days in America. Arrangements were made. Stepan would stay as our guest until he found work. Then he would pay two dollars a month rent.

That evening I was moved to a makeshift bed in the front room.

When Stephan was comfortably established in our house, Mama decided to put her culinary expertise to work. She allowed a few days to pass before approaching my father with her plan.

"Tonight," she ventured, "I will ask him to join us for supper. He always looks hungry — I think, where he works, they do not give him enough to eat."

"But he eats —"

"I know," Mama said impatiently. "But what can he eat there. A piece of bread with a slice of salami, and a pickle maybe. Is that food?"

That evening when our friend and "boarder" came home, my mother seated him at our table. "Stepan, will you share our supper with us?"

"Thank you, but already I —?"

"I know, you eat where you wash dishes. But, I ask you, what kind of job is that, anyway? Here in this neighborhood, on Eighty-third is a factory making automobiles — go there — I think they call it the Simplex — maybe they will take you."

With this, all resistance was overcome.

"And now, sit down, supper will get cold," Mama was filling his plate.

"Nobody could have been happier than my mother when, the following week Stepan announced that he had a job with the Simplex Auto Company, and was ready to have his meals with us.

And my mother had her first "paying" guest.

After that, the enterprise grew.

Some time later, our boarder surprised us with the news that he had invited a fellow Serbian, with whom he had become acquainted on the job, to share his Sunday dinner. Would Mama be so kind? Mama would, and she had another paying guest.

After much talk back and forth, with my father a most unwilling participant, it was decided to charge for extra supper thirty-five cents. Sunday dinner, which was a gala event, fifty cents.

Sunday dinner was indeed a festive affair, served in the front room on Mama's damask tablecloth, with napkins to match, as well as her fine flatware, a wedding present from her parents. The flatware had been lying in the pawnshop. "Now," Mama said, "I need the silver more than the money."

My mother's flatware, which she called "my silver," was always in and out of pawn in those days of small income. We lived on eight dollars a week — my father's salary — like most families in Yorkville. Two dollars had to be laid aside for the monthly rent of nine dollars. Even with milk four cents a quart and eggs ten cents a dozen, it was a tight economy. Sometimes the money ran out between paydays. Then my parents, like other immigrants, turned to the pawnshops which were so abundantly spread out along the streets at that time.

There they could meet the temporary need for ten cents, twenty-five cents, a dollar. Once when my mother wanted to go to the movies — the nickelodeon with a friend — she pawned a ring for ten cents. A few days later, she went back and got the ring.

I remember my mother running through the streets carrying a part of her trousseau, a feather bed, and a Turkish rug she had brought with her from the old country, for a temporary financial exchange with the pawnbroker when money ran out. Those things were then redeemed when the money was available. The pawnbroker, of course, had a charge for his services. If you did not pay the charges for a year, you lost your possessions.

The silver stayed out of the pawnshop. As admiration for my mother's culinary efforts grow, the evening suppers expanded to three or four. Dinners on Sunday sometimes saw five paying guests in the front room.

Mama was in her element. She loved these formal, quasi-social gatherings. "See," she said to Papa, "they eat good, and I have, besides the profit, a pleasure. What could be more wonderful?"

Papa had never been quite comfortable with dinner guests who settled a financial obligation before leaving. "Still, I am surprised that you would take money from friends, especially a friend from 'home'," he would say.

"But how long can a guest be a free guest? I love Stepan like a brother, but he must eat, and his friends, they must eat — and they must pay in restaurants. And God knows that junk they feed him. You must admit — in my kitchen they eat well — you can see for yourself that it has turned out to be a happy arrangement. And about the work, cooking, for me, is not work. Work is cleaning up after — and you can help, if it bothers you."

Papa laughed. "Well, if I must, I must. But I have one request. When we are alone, I will help. Before guests I don't put an apron on."

My mother promised to be the hostess until the "guests" left the house if Papa played host more graciously. This was promised as well.

My contribution was to set and clear the table, peel potatoes, and help with whatever Mama expected of me in her kitchen. Every Friday the noodle board was placed on the table. First I made the dough: two cups of flour, two eggs, an eggshell full of water, or drop by drop, as needed. I laid the dough aside for a while and then went back to it. A noodle board was placed on the table, a small box under my feet, and I was ready. I rolled the dough out with the rolling pin into three thin circles of dough about ten inches in diameter, then floured them very lightly, rolled them up, and cut each roll into quarter-inch-wide slices. Unrolled, and voila — noodles.

There were thin noodles for soup, wide ones for stew,

and still larger ones for Kugel, not to mention one-and-one-half inch squares for tarts. Mama would fill the squares with meat or apples, nuts and raisins, fold them into triangles and pinch the edges closed. Then, cooked in boiling water and served with meat gravy over the meat-filled triangles or a dusting of powdered sugar and cinnamon for the apple, nut and raisin tarts. Mouthwatering.

That was my job every Friday. Thin noodles for soup, square pieces for tarts, wider noodles for stews and chicken paprikasch. I must admit I did not care too much for the noodle-making enterprise. But how lucky for me. Those periods I spent in my mother's kitchen were pure gold. How I wish I could have understood their value then. I would not have bemoaned my fate so hard, on those afternoons when my friends were outside having fun.

How I remember it all. The marvelous smells permeating our rooms before supper; coming home, being aware, as I climbed up three flights of stairs, of mouthwatering, wonderful smells of good things being prepared.

And all our food was prepared with loving care and enormous effort. My mother did not buy chickens wrapped up shiny and clean in cellophane, weighed, priced and ready for the pot. She went to the market, selected a live chicken and had it butchered to be prepared further at home. In those days there were live chickens in markets for the housewife to select. Sometimes they came in wooden cages about a foot high,

666666666

stacked. I imagine there were about a dozen birds in each cage. Other times the chickens ran around in large pens. Why the chickens had to be bought alive, I have no idea. Perhaps the battle of the budget had something to do with it. They certainly had a good flavor, freshly killed.

I remember the process of selecting the live chicken — plump, but not too plump; too plump meant an old bird. Then came the butchering — off with the head. That cost five cents; or you took the chicken home and did it yourself. Then came the plucking — unless one wanted to pay the plucker for his services — ten cents. Mama did her own. A quick dip into boiling water to remove the last vestige of feathers after the plucking, then singeing over an open flame to make doubly certain.

A special Sunday treat for the boarders was palacsinta — a wonderful Hungarian pancake like crepe suzettes. For this Mama used: two eggs, three tablespoons of flour, one-half cup of milk, a little vanilla, some grated lemon or orange rind, and sugar to taste. Beat into a smooth batter, flowing like thick, sweet cream. Ladle a small amount onto a hot, lightly butter griddle and tilt back and forth until the mixture has spread evenly into a thin layer. When browned, turn to the other side just to set, immediately remove to a hot plate, spread with jam or finely ground nuts and sugar, and roll into a long curl. Lay side by side on a serving dish. Cover with a wine sauce or lemon sauce. It is absolutely delightful eating.

After dinner on Sunday afternoon people sometimes

dropped in. Nowadays people do not go visiting unless they call first, but then there were no telephones except in rich houses. If our friends in the building or across the street felt like seeing us, they came over. Whenever these new Americans came together there was one subject of conversation — the old country. The ladies would sit in the front room and talk. The men sat at the kitchen table and played cards. As evening approached, my mother would say, "Why don't you have supper with us."

And out of nothing would emerge a marvelous repast. Mama would gather leftovers such as cooked potatoes — cut them into small strips — add whatever meat and vegetables remained in the icebox, then add boiled eggs, mashed. Mix with sour cream and grated cheese, cover with buttered bread crumbs and bake about ten minutes in a hot oven. Delicious.

There is a sad ending to the story of Stepan. Several years later, in the fall of 1913, he was obliged to go back to his homeland. His brother had been inducted into the army, his elderly mother could not cope with the farm alone. Would the older son come home?

"As soon as order is restored, I will be back in America and will become a citizen," Stepan promised. And in our house there was an emptiness.

There came a letter. "No place like America," Stepan wrote, "I will be back."

But we never saw our surrogate relative again.

Stepan was one of the nearly one million Serbian men who were killed in the war in 1914.

10

The Hudson-Fulton Parade

The year was 1909.

We were settled in that modern tenement in Eighty-first Street. The additional two-dollars-a-month rent for the modern facilities, which Mama enjoyed so much, kept us pretty much at home. Outside activity cost money. It was not an option for the immigrant, with heads of most households earning seven or eight dollars a week.

Even five cents for carfare was a subject of discussion, when Papa took the elevated to work.

"Five cents you spend every day in this good weather,

when you can walk," Mama would say. "I can buy a bread and have one cent left over."

One cent bought a half pint of milk, an egg, a roll. So Papa walked to his job on "good" days.

In time Mama became involved with neighbors, who filled out our austere social life. All her friends lived within a block or two. Mama saw America only as Eighty-first Street between First Avenue and the East River. South of Seventy-ninth Street and west of Second Avenue didn't exist for her. The grocer, the butcher, Goodman's Drug Store, Paprika Weiss' Hungarian grocery — these were her ports of call when she went out. For her it was a major social event to go shopping in the neighborhood.

Then suddenly, outside activity of the most marvelous kind came our way. The State of New York decided upon a celebration commemorating the double anniversary of the discovery of the Hudson River by Henry Hudson in 1609 and the first voyage of Robert Fulton's steamship, the Clermont, up the Hudson to Albany in 1807. It was seven years in the planning and included a great procession of ships up the Hudson, a military parade, and an historical parade in Manhattan.

Well, my father was not going to ignore an event of such fascinating dimensions. All that year we lived with excerpts from the *Staats-Zeitung*, the German-language paper Papa read. We learned about Father Knickerbocker, said to be the patron saint of New York, the purchase of Manhattan for twenty-four dollars, the saga of Hiawatha.

If we had any doubts about the tremendous impact of that event on my father, they disappeared when at five in the morning, on the day of the great historical parade, he rousted us out of bed.

"Get up, time to get up!" he cried. "We are going to the Park to see the historical parade. And put on something warm. We will be sitting on a stone wall." This was October 2, 1909.

Mama came in with long winter underwear. I said, "Stones? What stones?" Mama said, "Your father is crazy. But anyway you should wear this, before you catch cold there in the park. this early in the morning."

"But it is not winter," I protested. "It's like summer yet."

"Basta!" Papa said. "Do what your mother says."

I did as I was told.

Thus fortified we started out, Papa loaded with blankets, Mama carrying a basket filled with liverwurst sandwiches, a few pickles, a huge container of coffee, and butter cookies. When Papa, laughing, thought that it was not the best of American customs to pack such a big lunch, Mama said, "Now I know why everyone outside Yorkville is skin and bones. Anyway," she added, "God knows how long the parade will continue, and one can get very hungry sitting out in the fresh air."

Street lamps were still lighted as we made our way the seven long blocks to Fifth Avenue and crossed through Central Park to the West Side and Central Park West. Surprisingly, we had company. Other early birds had beaten us to it. They made room for us on the stone wall on the edge of the Park and soon we became the best of companions, intent on the same mission.

My father's five A.M. foresight had not been so foolish after all. Other fathers had turned families out of bed at that unearthly hour.

Dawn brought the glow of the morning sun, with Mama fussing to keep me warm and well fed. All about us, throngs began to fill every available space. Children, hoisted on fathers' shoulders, awaited the big event with eager faces.

We had not anticipated that we would be sitting on the wall for six hours. But everyone took it in stride. Already we had consumed our lunch, when suddenly the parade band could be heard in the distance. It was one o'clock.

Mounted police in high regalia preceeded the procession. I remember many bands, then the great event — float after float depicting the critical episodes in the history of our adopted country. As we watched the parade, my father said, "This is wonderful. Today, all the world is represented here. From one end of the world to the other we came, together, to build this country." Mama nodded her head. "And without a doubt," my father went on, "the events that are being celebrated here today, Henry Hudson with his ship, the Half Moon, and Robert Fulton with his ship — the first steamship to go on the Hudson River — show us the history of the new land from three hundred years ago until today." Mama nodded her head again.

The floats made a tremendous impression on me. I still remember them. The different periods, going back three centuries, were represented. The Indians, then the Dutch, the English, among other European nations, the American Revolution, the Statue of Liberty commemorating the immigrant period that brought us to these shores.

One float after another showed marvelous scenes of legend and history. Father Knickerbocker, the patron saint of New York, stood, a benign figure, welcoming all who arrived from the four corners of the world to these shores. Then came the frightening "Headless Horseman," who pursued Ichabod Crane on his horse in the Legend of Sleepy Hollow. Then bowling on Bowling Green; Nathan Hale; President Washington taking the oath of office.

Much of it we didn't understand, but what wonderful bits of Americana these were for the newcomers around the turn of the century. The vessels, Half Moon and the Clermont, on their floats, seemed small and insignificant to have come down through history with such great achievements to their credit. I learned later that the Half Moon was only sixty-three feet long.

Unfortunately, Captain Hudson came to a sad end. In 1611 his crew mutinied and set the poor man adrift. He was never heard of again. The float showed two polar bears looking down on the poor man struggling through the ice.

I still have a vivid memory of the floats of the Indian

period: the figure of Hiawatha, tall, handsome, with his beautiful daughter in their canoe, bearing gifts for the Iroquois chief; Indian war dances; the five chiefs of the Iroquois nation as they disappeared slowly into the distance to make room for yet other pieces of Americana, portraying bits and pieces of the past.

At the end, tired, sleepy, I walked home with my parents. The Hudson-Fulton Parade. I never forgot it.

The parade started at 1 PM from 110th Street and Central Park West. People had been waiting since daybreak.

More than a million
people watched. It
was the greatest
parade in the history
of New York.

"The Car Luxurious"
TOWN CAR
EARN
Goods 14th
ANYTIME
SHREDDED WHEAT
BISCUIT
THE NATIONAL SODA CRACK
Uneeda
Biscuit
NATIONAL BISCUIT COMPANY
CADILLAC

The parade
moved down
Central Park West,
across Columbus
Circle...

...and then down Fifth Avenue. The photograph shows the full-scale replica of Henry Hudson's ship, the Half Moon.

129

Our Indian heritage was a prominent theme in the parade. Floats commemorated the Legend of Hiawatha and the purchase of Manhattan in 1626 from Indian chiefs for the equivalent of twenty-four dollars. That amount, invested at six percent compounded, would be approximately thirty billion dollars today — greater than the value of all Manhattan real estate.

131

11
Elections

$\mathcal{W}$hen the newcomer landed
in Battery Park his first need was to find shelter among
people of similar cultures and backgrounds, who spoke
his language. Some countries provided immigrants in
sufficient numbers to form substantial enclaves of their
own kind — Little Italy, Chinatown or the Jewish neigh-
borhoods of the Lower East Side.

My mother had other ideas. "Now we are in
America," she said, "I want to live among Americans."
So the Greenfield family, in its flight from toilets down
three flights of stairs and other such indignities, found

its niche, after trial and error, on Eighty-first Street in the Yorkville section of New York. There we flourished. On Eighty-first Street, near the East River, where Mama happily settled us, we became part of the blend of cultures, creeds and backgrounds that was Yorkville in my time. The whole world seemed to be represented, certainly all of Europe, with the German language predominating. The melting pot worked for them all, drawing them into that marvelous American amalgamation of peoples from different lands.

Now, as I look back to that period, I can understand the reason for the tremendous value the newcomers placed on elections and, above all, the concept of the common man electing his president. This, my father never, in his entire life, had experienced. "I can even elect a president," he would write home with pride when he first came to America. In his part of Europe, the privilege of choosing a high government official, let alone a president, was unheard of. "Nobody has a voice in the government where I come from. No one elects anybody," I would hear, "Not a president, not a king, not a dogcatcher even."

To become an American citizen, so he could vote, was the greatest of my father's dreams. Joseph Resch, our landlord, had been an immigrant like ourselves some twenty years before. In him my father saw the promise of his new country as well as its possibilities. "Look where he is," Papa would exclaim. "He owns this house, he owns the beer saloon in it; and he is a big man in politics."

One day in 1912, after the required five-year waiting period, Papa became a citizen of the United States. With him, the entire family became citizens also, according to the law at that time.

Toward evening, neighbors came to congratulate the family. Certainly, our friends would not let as important an event as our citizenship go unrecognized. Mama was in her element. The coffeepot was steaming, cake had been cut into serving pieces, and a nice bouquet of flowers from Mr. Resch decorated the front room. And, of course, neither did my mother forget that in my father's new status as a citizen her high hopes for the better life had finally come to fruition.

My mother always thought of citizenship as the door to a better economic situation. Time passed. Nothing changed. My father's salary stayed the same. Six months later, with her fifteenth wedding anniversary nearing, she faced my father. "Now we are here five years and nothing has changed. You did not get a raise, and your citizenship has not done much for me either." After a pause, she added, "It seems to me that for you it has given satisfaction. For me, there is still so little money. I still have to give a story to the grocer, when I have to pay something that is more important; your lodge dues I had to take care of so they take care of us, God forbid something happens. And when I pay the grocer, then the shoemaker has to wait and I have to wear slippers all day. I tell you, I am disappointed. What is the use of being a citizen, when for the family nothing has changed?"

Papa smiled. "Come, sit down, I will tell you about citizenship. Patiently Papa explained that being a citizen had nothing to do with family finances. "It is important for other reasons. It is important for voting. It gives an ordinary man a chance to decide who will be his president. A real mensch, a man is in America," my father said. And no bigger tribute could be offered by Papa than that simple word "mensch."

Our friends shared Papa's pride in the act of voting. Elections were a festive occasion in our neighborhood. Election eve was celebrated with torchlight parades, bonfires and block parties. Citizens and citizens-to-be would gather in the streets.

Bonfires played a big role in the celebration. There were enormous fires fifteen to twenty feet high. The boys in the neighborhood started to collect wood ten days before. Wooden signs and pushcarts disappeared from the streets. If any were left out, the boys took them.

Many a kitchen lost a wooden utensil to the election fires. When complaints from housewives came to Papa's ears he would say, "Let them have it. It is a small price to pay to celebrate the election of a president. It is for a good cause."

As darkness approached people began assembling for the celebration, joining in the parade or the general hilarity of the block party. The German band began to play. They were not always Germans, but we always called street musicians "the German band."

With the setting sun we could hear distant drums

beating the election message, heralding the torchlight parade, weaving its way slowly through neighborhood streets, torches held high. Leading the parade was our landlord, Mr. Resch. He towered over his fellow marchers. Mr. Resch was the captain of our precinct and the most important man in our neighborhood.

Now politics came into play. The musicians stopped playing, and men in spats and bowler hats and striped vests made speeches standing on soap boxes on street corners. People crowded around our landlord, slapped his back, yelled over heads, "Hi-ya, Joe." One of the spats-and-bowler-hats shouted, "Great turnout here!" "Hey," another bowler hat cried, "Heard ya have a couple who got their second papers!"

Mr. Resch waved and laughed his greetings in return. He was standing beside the steps going into our building, where a table had been placed and beer and sandwiches were dispensed. Refreshments had been donated by Mr. Resch who owned the beer saloon in the building.

Two other families, besides ourselves, became citizens in that period. Three more Democrats, three more votes for Mr. Resch.

The author and her father in 1912.

Joseph Resch, a successful businessman and Democratic politician, was the hero of the neighborhood. Most immigrants in Yorkville voted Democratic.

Voting was by hand-marked ballot in 1912.

Waiting for returns on election night in 1910. In an era before radio and television, there was no other way to get the results quickly.

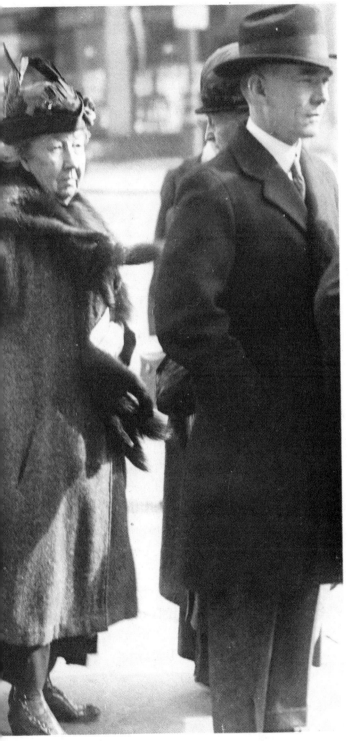

Some of the first
women voters.
in America.
A constitutional
amendment
allowed women
to vote in 1920
for the first time.

143

12
The Great War

In 1914, a group of Serbian
nationalists assassinated the heir to the Hapsburg
throne, Archduke Franz Ferdinand of Austria, and his
wife, in the town of Sarajevo in Serbia. The assassination embroiled the world in a war that was destined to
go into four years of bitter fighting, and eventually
brought the United States into the fray.

It was a war to end all wars.

Two mighty groups of nations faced each other that
summer in 1914 — the Allies against the Central
Powers. For us in Yorkville, the lines were more simply
drawn. It was Germany against Great Britain.

Communications closed between the two worlds, causing great hardship among the many European nationals living in our neighborhood. My mother was devastated. Her entire family lived in Serbia, in the midst of the conflict. Bulgarian, German and Austrian armies marched and counter-marched across the ruined land. The Serbian army fought with incredible valor, but it was heavily outnumbered. Many lives were lost.

"My God!" my mother exclaimed, "How will it all end?"

Papa consoled her. "It cannot last long, three months, at most." But Mama was not reassured. "How can you say that?" she cried. "The whole world in Europe is in this terrible bloodshed. They are crazy there in Europe . . . The Kaiser and his Junkers will not give up their dream. And my family is in the middle of it. My God! The first thing they do, they kill —"

"Now you are being silly," Papa broke in. "This is the twentieth century."

"Well, my smart husband, if we are in this advanced civilization, why are people still killing each other?"

"The answer is, of course, I don't know."

Shaking her head, Mama said nothing, but her eyes had been filling. And so we waited out the great war, which was to end all wars.

New York City, with its varied population of immigrants, was in a quandary. People with ties in the old country took sides, in their homes, in the streets, in the press. Our Yorkville neighborhood was a mixture mostly of Germans, Czechs, Austrians, and a few Hungarians. It was largely a German-speaking population. Pro-German views were decidedly popular. Those with Allied sympathies had the dilemma every day of deciding whether or not to get involved in the heated discussions.

In our house, my parents had strong convictions about this war. My father was pro-German in the beginning. He had lived in Germany, he spoke German, he had the old-world respect for authority and the Kaiser. My mother thought the war barbaric and sinful. "In this twentieth century," she cried, "that grown-up people should kill each other when they don't even know why, is something that I will never understand." And she extracted a promise from my father that he would keep his opinions to himself.

But in 1915 came the tragedy of the sinking of the Lusitania off the coast of Ireland, by a German submarine. America was in an uproar. Headlines screamed their outrage. "THE SINKING OF THE LUXURY LINER, LUSITANIA, WAS DELIBERATE MURDER!" Many were for an immediate declaration of war. Angry discussions developed in our street over the terrible loss of more than eleven hundred lives, and President Wilson's neutrality "after the Lusitania outrage." My parents deplored the continued pro-German sentiment and the justifications for the sinking of the luxury liner. There were many apologists for the indiscrminate U-boat attacks by Germany. Across the nation, divergent factions created their own little wars — Germany against Great Britain, the Central Powers against the Allies.

All eyes were on President Wilson. Theodore Roosevelt said we owed it to our self-respect to take action against the German nation. "It is inconceivable for America not to take appropriate measures . . . We can no longer remain neutral spectators." said the ex-president.

But despite all the clamor, Wilson was determined to remain neutral.

With time heads cooled, as the President expected, and with war averted, the country, in a turnabout, saw in President Wilson's stand "a magnificent restraint." Papa said, "The President knows what he is doing." The nation agreed.

But in our house there was disillusionment with Germany. "How could a civilized country, like Germany, do such a thing?" my mother cried. "Eleven hundred people drowning — so many lives lost — and for what?" my mother went on. "God knows what else we can expect from this terrible war." As far as she was concerned, none of the combatants in Europe had any justification for the bloodshed.

"I wish somebody would already give in," she would say in her exasperation. "What is the fighting for, anyway? What will it come to, when it is all over?"

"Well, for one thing, we will get mail from your family again," Papa said.

"You! You are always joking," Mama cried, not in a joking mood. "What if this country gets into it?"

"Don't worry," Papa interrupted. "There will be no war. We will never be in it — not with a president like Wilson. He is the peace President."

"But, the sinking of the Lusitania — and from what I heard, many American ships, the submarines are sinking. How can we not be drawn into this way?"

"There will be no war in this part of the world," Papa repeated. "The President, he is a man of his word. He will find some way to deal with the German war machine without getting us into it."

Mama sighed. "I don't know — so many ships sunk already — and a whole year already I have no mail from home."

"I know it is hard for you," Papa consoled my mother. "But how much longer can this last?"

"As long as Germany has a submarine to sink ships — and we will be in it, mark my words," said Mama. It was her way to tempt the fates into reverse reaction.

This was in the front room, after supper. My father was seated in his favorite rocking chair beside the window; Mama was sitting at the round oak table, darning needle and sock in hand.

After supper, in our house, was discussion time.

Suddenly my father rose from his rocking chair. "I'm going down for some fresh air . . ." When my mother remained silent, he added, "I'll be back soon."

"You are going down to talk about the Lusitania?" There was strong opposition in my mother's voice.

Papa laughed. "You know me like a book — all right — so I'm going down to get things cleared up with our neighbors."

"Well," Mama said, "maybe the sinking will bring some to their senses. But anyway, be careful what you say —"

"I will say what is on my mind. That is what I will say," Papa exploded. "It's a free country — and don't worry so much — so I'll keep my mouth shut, after I —"

Mama laughed. "That I would like to believe."

"There is no pleasing you."

"All right, Mama said in her worried tone. "Go down. Only be careful what you say."

"Why — I would like to know? They are our friends.?"

"Our former friends, who are now pro-German — and maybe, they will not like to hear any more what you have to say."

"Well, it's a free country, thank God," Papa said again, going toward the door.

"A terrible thing, the sinking," a neighbor said, when my father joined the group that had congregated on the steps of our tenement. "An act of barbarism, that's what is was," my father cried.

"But in war, one must expect such things. People should stay home," another voice said — "Germany had a right —"

"What right?" An angry, tell-tale red crossed Papa's face, as forgetting his good intentions, he gave vent to his feelings. "Maybe a right to kill women and children?

149

My God! Eleven hundred people drowned when the Lusitania was attacked by that submarine! How can you, my friends, stand there, and spout such outrageous apologies for the Kaiser's war machine. And I'll tell you this, here and now — if the Central Powers have to rely on this kind of weapon to win the war, I feel sorry for them when the struggle finally comes to an end. Only God can help them then."

And my father reminded the crowd that had gathered, "In the city, people are calling for war. Germany must be restrained, they say. For God's sakes, do any of you want war to come to our shores? And if these sinkings continue, I think even the President will not be strong enough to keep us out of it."

"Then why don't people stay home?" Mr. Rothblatt of the top floor said. "They have no business in a war zone."

"Dummkopf!" Papa shouted, forgetful of his good intentions. "Off the coast of Ireland the ship was attacked! Is that a war zone?" Papa terminated the argument.

At home, my father had hardly opened the door, when my mother, giving vent to her fears, descended upon him with full force.

"Now you did it!" she cried. "You had to open your mouth, when it would do no good anyway." Why can't you just stay out of it? my mother said, "— or at least, if you must, say something unoffensive to them."

"All right," my father said, "so I talked. But I tell you this, my dear wife, with our pro-German neighbors,

everything they don't agree with is offensive. Nobody is
neutral here. I found that out."

The fact was that New York was by this time pro-
Allied. Only in our neighborhood did pro-German sentiment still prevail.

That November, Wilson ran for his second term. In
our house, Election Day always was a time of excite-
ment. This particular day, when my father dressed in
his Sunday best to vote for the Herr Professor, there
was something in the air, for my mother dressed as well.
"I want to go with you," she said. "I want to see how
this Election Day is working. Maybe, some day, ladies
will vote too."

Papa laughed. "You are being silly. Women have not
the understanding of politics, to vote."

"All right, maybe not. But I want to go with you."

That day, the day Wilson was elected to a second
term on his peace platform, my mother proudly accompanied my father to the polling booth.

And the struggle in Europe went on, into the third
year — a struggle no one had dreamed would last more
than three months.

In February, Congress passed a resolution asking
American citizens to heed the submarine menace, and
keep off the ships of belligerents.

This drove Senator Stone of Missouri into opposition. "I shall do everything in my power," he declared, "
to keep the United States out of this conflict across the
ocean but, I cannot, in good conscience, abridge the

rights of American citizens to exercise their free right of travel . . . It would be a deep humiliation for the nation. Further humiliation would surely follow."

And humiliation did indeed follow for my father, for what my mother had feared came to pass. Papa came home one evening holding a blood-soaked handkerchief over his face.

"My God! What did they do to you? My mother reacted in her usual uninhibited way.

"Calm yourself," Papa said. "It's nothing. I have no idea why my nose should have acted up this way. Maybe I have high blood pressure."

"Or maybe," my mother broke in, "a strange fist came out of the air accidentally — or could it be that maybe you talked too much? Always I said, keep your feelings to yourself. This is no time to be a hero."

Poor Papa, changing napkins to stop the flow of blood from the injured nose, took his scolding in silence. And he ate his supper without a word; not that he had anything to say. He knew, of course, that Mama had guessed correctly.

The U-boat attacks upon our merchant ships were bringing us ever closer to war. But, determined to keep his election pledge, the President decided to continue to deal with these developing crises in his usual diplomatic way. It was, however, evident, in the course of time, that Germany had no intention of ceasing U-boat warfare.

Finally, President Wilson ordered the arming of American merchant vessels with naval crews and guns.

The President said that to send unarmed merchant ships across the ocean had become totally unacceptable.

By February, 1917 the U-boats had sunk two hundred ships. Still Wilson stood firm in his neutrality; armed neutrality, yes, but not war.

Nevertheless, we were closer to war, and the country was increasingly impatient with Wilson's "armed neutrality." A minister in Brooklyn suggested that a tortoise should replace the eagle in the Great Seal of the United States.

Then it happened. On January 31, 1917, the Germans declared unrestricted submarine warfare. American passenger ships could still sail, but only under humiliating conditions. They could only sail to one British port, they could not deviate from a special course set by the Germans, and they had to paint stripes on their hulls and fly a checkered flag.

Still the President refused to act. Then he heard about the Zimmerman telegram. It was a message from Germany to the president of Mexico proposing that if war broke out between Germany and the United States, and Mexico entered the war on the German side, Germany would give her Arizona, New Mexico and Texas as a reward.

That did it. Our neutrality was at an end. This final outrage had provoked the wrath of America. The President was reluctant to the end; "It was just a choice of evils," he said. But the nation was infuriated by the news that Germany actually proposed to carve up the United States. "COUNTRY IN A MILITANT MOOD," a headline declared. On April 6, 1917, Congress declared war against Germany.

Almost immediately after, the President asked Congress to pass the Selective Service Act. All male citizens between the ages of twenty-one and thirty-one were ordered to register for the draft. On June 5, 1917, our young men stood in line to register.

There was consternation among immigrants with sons of draft age, those very sons of families with pro-European sympathies, now asked to fight kith and kin across the ocean.

In another of those spectacular metamorphoses that only America is capable of, the sons of European immigrants went off to camp in their new role as citizen soldiers. And when finally our New York boys embarked for France, singing, "Over There! Over There!" the metamorphosis of the parents was complete as well.

There were parents of all nations, of all faiths, all Americans; a grand melting pot of immigrants of the world, seeing their sons marching off, with a prayer in their hearts and a song on their lips.

"Over There! Over There! Send the Word Over There! The Yanks are Coming, The Yanks are Coming The Drums are Drumming Everywhere."

When I look back, what I remember best about that time were the songs. Without radio or television, we lived through the period in a wave of patriotic song and prayer. There were songs at Liberty Bond rallies and

scrap metal drives. There were hymns, recruiting songs
and war songs. There were patriotic songs in the streets,
in the army camps, in the theaters, on the stage with
George M. Cohan; all the time, throughout the country,
those mavelous melodies were borne on the winds
across the land.

How I remember that stuttering song,

"K-K-K-Katy, beautiful Katy!"

which gave way to the K.P. version the boys sang in the
camps.

"K-K-K-K.P., dirty old K.P.
That's the only army job that I abhor."

Then there was the stirring song,

"Over there! Over there!
Send the word, send the word, over there,
That the Yanks are coming, the Yanks are coming,
The drums are beating everywhere.
So prepare, say a prayer;
Send the word, send the word to beware;
We'll be over, we're coming over,
And we won't be back 'til it's over — over there."

And, of course,

"How ya gonna keep 'em down on the farm
After they've seen Paree?
How ya gonna keep 'em away from Broadway,
Jazzin' around, paintin' the town?"

Here is a nostalgic song,

> "Goodbye Ma! Goodbye Pa!
> Goodbye Mule, with yer old hee-haw!
> I may not know what this war's about;
> But you bet, by gosh, I'll soon find out;
> And oh my, sweetheart, don't you fear,
> I'll bring back the Kaiser for a souvenir!"

And here is the lament of the soldier whose locks are shorn.

> "Good morning, Mr. Zip, Zip, Zip,
> Get your hair cut just as short as mine!
> Good morning, Mr. Zip, Zip, Zip,
> You'll certainly not look fine!
> Good morning, Mr. Zip, Zip, Zip,
> With your hair cut just as short as mine.
> With your hair cut just as short as —
> Just as short as, just as short as, just as short as —
> Mine!"

It is just as essential," said General Leonard Wood, "that a soldier know how to sing, as how to carry a rifle, and how to shoot."

New York Times.

THE WEATHER
Local showers today; Tuesday, fair; fresh, shifting winds, becoming northwest.
For full weather report see Page 17.

ONE CENT In Greater New York, Jersey City and Newark. | Elsewhere TWO CENTS

Propose Pan-American Memorial to Columbus
A splendid tomb topped by a great light is proposed to be erected in Santo Domingo, in the Caribbean Sea, by subscriptions from peoples of all lands. See NEXT SUNDAY'S TIMES.

OUR GUNS FIRE ON SANTO DOMINGO

Few Shots from the Machias Stop Bombardment of Puerto Plata by President Bordas.

WARNED BY CAPT. RUSSELL

Told Not to Endanger Foreigners in Attack on Rebels There—Refugees Taken Off by Our Boats.

Special to The New York Times.
WASHINGTON, June 28.—Following general instructions from the Navy Department to protect the lives and property of Americans and foreigners in Santo Domingo, the little American gunboat Machias on Friday afternoon entered the inner harbor of Puerto Plata, and with a few shots from her main battery silenced a battery of President Bordas's forces that was bombarding the town.

The bombardment was in violation of emphatic orders from Capt. Russell, commanding the American squadron, that the attack on the city, which is in fume such ranks, be conducted in such a way as not to imperil the lives of foreigners.

Capt. Russell is in personal command of the first line battleship South Carolina, that was detached from service at Vera Cruz when conditions in Santo Domingo became threatening. His dispatches to the department, which, like all dispatches from Santo Domingo, took two days to come, makes no mention of casualties. His dispatch follows:

PUERTO PLATA, June 20, 1914.

$500,000 FIRE AT DOVER, N. J.

Incendiaries Destroy Richardson & Boynton Stove Plant.

DOVER, N. J., June 28.—All of the plant of the Richardson & Boynton Company, except the shipping department building, was destroyed by fire today. The fire manufactured stoves and ranges, and its plant, which was

---

HEIR TO AUSTRIA'S THRONE IS SLAIN WITH HIS WIFE BY A BOSNIAN YOUTH TO AVENGE SEIZURE OF HIS COUNTRY

Francis Ferdinand Shot During State Visit to Sarajevo.

TWO ATTACKS IN A DAY

Archduke Saves His Life First Time by Knocking Aside a Bomb Hurled at Auto.

SLAIN IN SECOND ATTEMPT

Lad Dashes at Car as the Royal Couple Return from Town Hall and Kills Both of Them.

LAID TO A SERVIAN PLOT

Heir Warned Not to Go to Bosnia, Where Populace Met Him with Servian Flags.

AGED EMPEROR IS STRICKEN

Shock of Tragedy Prostrates Francis Joseph—Young Assassin Proud of His Crime.

Special Cable to THE NEW YORK TIMES.
SARAJEVO, Bosnia, June 28. (By courtesy of the Vienna Neue Freie Presse.)—Archduke Francis Ferdinand, heir to the throne of Austria-Hungary, and his wife, the Duchess of Hohenberg, were shot and killed by a Bosnian student here today. The fatal shooting was the second attempt upon the lives of the couple during the day, and is believed to have been the result of a political conspiracy.

This morning, as Archduke Francis Ferdinand and the Duchess were driving to a reception at the Town Hall a bomb was thrown at their motor car. The Archduke pushed it off with his arm.

The bomb did not explode until after the Archduke's car had passed on, and the occupants of the next car, Count von Boos-Waldeck and Col. Morizzi, the Archduke's aide de camp, were slightly injured. Among the spectators, six persons were more or less seriously hurt.

The author of the attempt at assassination was a compositor named Gabrinovics, who comes from Trebinje.

After the attempt upon his life the Archduke ordered his car to halt, and after he found out who had happened he drove to the Town Hall, where the Town Councillors, with the Mayor at their head, awaited him. The Mayor was about to begin his address of welcome, when the Archduke interrupted him angrily, saying:

"Herr Burgermeister, it is perfectly outrageous! We have come to Sarajevo on a visit and have had a bomb thrown at us."

could only certify they were both dead.

The authors of both attacks upon the Archduke are born Bosnians. Gabrinovics is a compositor, and worked for a few weeks in the Government printing works at Belgrade. He returned to Sarajevo a Servian chauvinist, and made no concealment of his sympathies with the King of Servia. Both he and the actual murderer of the Archduke and the Duchess expressed themselves to the police in the most cynical fashion about their crimes.

ARCHDUKE IGNORED WARNING.

Servian Minister Feared Trouble if Heir Went to Bosnia.

Special Cable to THE NEW YORK TIMES.
(Dispatch to The London Daily Mail.)
VIENNA, June 28.—When the news of the assassination of the Archduke Francis Ferdinand and the Duchess was broken to the aged Emperor Francis Joseph he said: "Horrible, horrible! No sorrow is spared me."

The Emperor, whose yesterday left here for local, his favorite Summer resort, amid acclamations of the people, will return to Vienna at once, in spite of the hardship of the journey in the terrible heat.

The Archduke, who was created head of the army, went, to Bosnia to represent the Emperor at the grand manoeuvres there. This was the first time the Archduke had paid an official visit to Bosnia. The Emperor visited the provinces immediately after their annexation, in 1908, and the manner in which he mixed freely with the people was much criticised at the time, as those in his party were always afraid lest some Slav or Mohammedan fanatic might attempt the monarch's life. The Emperor's popularity, however, saved him from all danger of this kind.

Before the Archduke went to Bosnia last Wednesday the Servian Minister here expressed doubt as to the wisdom of the journey, saying the country was in a very turbulent condition and the Servian part of the populatio.. might organise a demonstration against the Archduke. The Minister said if the Archduke went himself he certainly

by splinters from the bomb. Several persons on the pavement were very seriously hurt by the explosion of the bomb, which was thrown by a young man named Tabrinovitch, (Gabrinovics,) who is a typist from Trebenje, in Herzegovina, and is of Servian nationality. He was arrested some twenty minutes later.

The Archduke and his wife left the Town Hall, intending to visit those who had been injured by the bomb, when a schoolboy 19 years old, named Prinzip, who came from Grahovo, fired a shot at the Archduke's head. The boy fired from the shelter of a projecting house.

Wore Bullet-Proof Coat.

The boy must have been carefully instructed in his part, for it was a well-marked secret that the Archduke always wore a coat of silk strands which were woven obliquely, so that no weapon or bullet could pierce it. It once saw a strip of this fabric used for a motor-car tire, and it was puncture-proof. This new invention enabled the Archduke to brave attempts on his life, but his head naturally was uncovered.

The Duchess was shot in the body. The boy fired several times, but only two shots took effect. The Archduke and his wife were carried to the Konak, or palace, in a dying condition.

Later details show that the assassin darted forth from his hiding place behind a house and actually got on the motor car in which the Archduke and his wife were sitting. He took close aim first at the Archduke, and then at the Duchess. The fact that no one stopped him, and that he was allowed to perpetrate the dastardly act indicate that the conspiracy was carefully planned and that the Archduke fell a victim to a political plot. The aspiration of the Servian population in Bosnia to join with Servia and form a great Servian kingdom is well known. No doubt today's assassination was regarded as a means of forwarding this plan.

Break News to Children.

The Archduke's children are at Gluines, in Bohemia, and relatives already have left Vienna to break the news to them. The Duke of Cumberland motored to Ischl immediately upon receipt of the news and has received the Emperor, who will arrive in Vienna at 6 o'clock tomorrow. The bodies of the Archduke and his wife will not be brought to Vienna until tomorrow a week.

it is feared that it will lead to serious complications with the unruly kingdom, and may have far-reaching results. The future of the empire is a subject of general discussion. It is felt that the Servians have been treated too leniently, and some hard words are being said about the present foreign policy.

All the public buildings are draped in long black streamers and the flags are all at half-mast.

BRAVERY OF ARCHDUKE.

Gave First Aid to Those Wounded by the Bomb.

SARAJEVO, Bosnia, June 28.—Archduke Francis Ferdinand, heir to the Austro-Hungarian throne, and the Duchess of Hohenberg, his morganatic wife, were shot dead in the main street of the Bosnian capital by a student today while they were making an apparently triumphant progress through the city on their annual visit to the annexed provinces of Bosnia and Herzegovina.

The Archduke was hit full in the face and the Duchess was shot through the abdomen and throat. Their wounds proved fatal within a few minutes after they reached the palace, whence they were hurried with all speed.

Those responsible for the assassination took care that it would prove effective, as there were two assailants, the first armed with a bomb and the other with a revolver. The bomb was thrown at the royal automobile as it was proceeding to the Town Hall, where a reception was to be held, but the Archduke saw the deadly missile coming and warded it off with his arm. It fell outside the car and exploded, slightly wounding two aids de camp in a second car, and half a dozen spectators. It was on the return of the procession that the tragedy was added to the long list of those that have darkened the pages of the recent history of the Hapsburgs.

As the royal automobile reached a prominent point in the route to the palace, an eighth grade student, Gavrio Prinzip, sprang out of the crowd and poured a fusillade of bullets from an automatic pistol at the Archduke and the Duchess. Both fell mortally wounded.

Wards Off the Bomb.

The first attempt against the Archduke occurred just outside the Girls' High School. The Archduke's car had restart-

The Archduke
Ferdinand and his
wife enter their car
in Sarajevo on
June 28, 1914. They
were shot and
killed ten minutes
later.

159

The maiden voyage of the Lusitania, largest ship afloat when launched. She was sunk on May 7, 1915, with loss of 1198 lives.

"All the News That's Fit to Print."

The New Yor

VOL. LXIV...NO. 20,923. · · · · ·

NEW YORK, SATURDAY, MAY 8, 1915.-

LUSITANIA SUNK BY A SUBMARINE,
TWICE TORPEDOED OFF IRISH CO.
CAPT. TURNER SAVED, FROHMA.
WASHINGTON BELIEVES THAT

SHOCKS THE PRESIDENT

Washington Deeply Stirred by the Loss of American Lives.

BULLETINS AT WHITE HOUSE

Wilson Reads Them Closely, but Is Silent on the Nation's Course.

HINTS OF CONGRESS CALL

Loss of Lusitania Recalls Firm Tone of Our First Warning to Germany.

CAPITAL FULL OF RUMORS

Reports That Liner Was to be Sunk Were Heard Before Actual News Came.

Special to The New York Times.

WASHINGTON, May 7. — Never since that April day, three years ago, when word came that the Titanic had gone down, has Washington been so stirred as it is tonight over the sinking of the Lusitania. The early reports told that there had been no loss of life, but the relief that these advices caused gave way to the greatest concern late this evening when it became known that there had been many deaths. Although they are profoundly reticent, officials realize that this tragedy, involving the loss of American citizens, is likely to bring about a crisis in the international relations of the United States.

It is pointed out that the sinking of the Lusitania is the outcome of a series of incidents that have been the cause of concern to this Government in its endeavor to maintain a strictly neutral position in the great European war.

The Lost Cunard Steamsh
X Where the First Torpedo Struck.   XX Where t

Cunard Office Here Besieged for News; Fate of 1,918 on Lusitania Long in Doubt

Nothing Heard from the Well-Known Passengers on Board—Story of Disaster Long Unconfirmed While Anxious Crowds Seek Details.

Official news of the sinking of the Lusitania yesterday reached New York in fragmentary reports, and several hours elapsed between the first unveri-

dently a distress call from the liner, which said:

Come at once. Big list. Position ten miles west Kinsale.

List of Saved Includes Capt. Vanderbilt and Frohman

LONDON, Saturday, May 8.- 5:30 A. M.—
received from the British Admiralty at Queer
all the torpedo boats and tugs and armed trawle
which went out from Queenstown to the relief
returned.

These vessels have landed 505 survivors and
more survivors are reported aboard a steamer, w
five bodies have been landed at Kinsale, making
survivors 658, besides forty-five dead. The number
and it is considered possible Kinsale fishing boats

Times.

EXTRA 5:30 A.M.

Weather Today and Sunday, Fair.

PAGES.   ONE CENT   In Greater New York, } Elsewhere Jersey City and Newark. } TWO CENTS.

BABLY 1,260 DEAD;
SINKS IN 15 MINUTES;
VANDERBILT MISSING;
RAVE CRISIS IS AT HAND

...truck.

Saw the Submarine 100 Yards Off and Watched Torpedo as It Struck Ship

Ernest Cowper, a Toronto Newspaper Man, Describes Attack, Seen from Ship's Rail—Poison Gas Used in Torpedoes, Say Other Passengers.

Queenstown, Saturday, May 8, 3:18 A. M.

in an orderly, prompt, and efficient manner. Miss Helen Smith appealed to me to save

SOME DEAD TAKEN ASHORE

Several Hundred Survivors at Queenstown and Kinsale.

STEWARD TELLS OF DISASTER

One Torpedo Crashes Into the Doomed Liner's Bow, Another Into the Engine Room.

SHIP LISTS OVER TO PORT

Makes It Impossible to Lower Many Boats, So Hundreds Must Have Gone Down.

ATTACKED IN BROAD DAY

Passengers at Luncheon—Warning Had Been Given by Germans Before the Ship Left New York.

Only 650 Were Saved, Few Cabin Passengers

QUEENSTOWN, Saturday, May 8, 4:28 A. M.—Survivors of the Lusitania who have arrived here estimate that only about 650 of those aboard the steamer were saved, and say only a small proportion of those rescued were saloon passengers.

Official Confirmation

WASHINGTON, May 8. —A dispatch to the State Department early today from American Consul Lauriet at Queenstown stated that the total num-

The sinking of the Lusitania by a German U-boat was a fateful step in America's move toward war.

163

13
War Comes to America

*W*hen President Wilson asked Congress to declare war on Germany in 1917, the country accepted without question his statement that war was unavoidable, now that the German government had departed from "humane practices of civilized nations" and started "a war against mankind."

At the same time the President called for war with justice, and without the fruits of victory.

It was an impossible order. The mood of America was ugly.

Thousands of European nationals were living in

America. The Alien and Sedition laws were passed in June, 1917 as a defensive measure against possible sabotage. War fever brought injustice and hardship, and often arrests upon the flimsiest of suspicions. Anything German was re-named. I remember the German Hospital became "The Lenox Hill Hospital." Sauerkraut changed into liberty cabbage, frankfurters became hot dogs and hamburgers were now Salisbury steak. Pretzels were thrown off the free lunch counters.

And the fresh American Expeditionary Forces gave new heart to the exhausted Allies. Winston Churchill wrote later of "this seemingly inexhaustible flood of gleaming youths." They arrived just in time. The German army attacked in the spring of 1918, in a last desperate effort to win the war before the strength of the American forces was felt. The Germans came within sixty miles of Paris and then they were stopped. Many precious lives would be lost in the coming months, but the Germans had already lost the war.

Meanwhile, President Wilson defined his terms for peace. "The war must be ended in terms that would create a peace worth preserving." Throughout the world the imminent cessation of four years of fighting was hailed with wild demonstrations of thankfulness and joy.

On November 9, 1918, the Kaiser abdicated and fled to Holland.

On November eleventh an armistice was signed. The war was over.

New York went into a wild frenzy of celebration. People streamed out of their homes to join the jubilant crowds, with noise-makers, with shouts of relief, with song, or just to be part of the historical, never-to-be-forgotten moment. Crowding Broadway, they pressed through the streets shoulder to shoulder, while the auto horns blared their din.

Open house in our neighborhood was no less noisy, with friends and neighbors exhanging cheers and milling about in and out of homes. For the moment all hostility was put aside. In his saloon Mr. Resch donated beer. My mother served coffee and cake.

That winter we saw a great deal of snow. People were holed up in their homes with very few outside contacts, except for chance meetings on the street when, with coat collars turned up and hats turned down against the wind, few words were exchanged, if any. Communication between people came almost to a halt, since there was not one telephone in the street. Information on the peace settlements was nil, without radios or other electronic communications. Now Christmas passed, going into New Year, 1919, without undue post-war incident.

I remember my father saying, "Well, it looks to me that the war, with its by-product, the pro and con issues, has been put to rest, at last."

My mother said, "The first winter with peace. It will be a good New Year for people."

Finally, the end of winter cleared the streets of New York of snow and sleet. The spring sun warmed our bones, brought life into the neighborhood, and also the dreary news that second thoughts indeed were stirring.

It came to us like a bolt out of the blue.

My mother was having her usual mid-afternoon coffee with her friend Anna Wagner, and as I did not go to work that day for some reason, I naturally took part in the coffee klatch. Mama was bringing the Streussel Kuchen to the table, when the bell rang. It was our next-door neighbor.

Mama set the cake down. "Come in, how nice to see you. Come, sit down, have a coffee with us. You know each other." Mrs. Wagner nodded. Our neighbor, saying, "How are you, Mrs. Wagner," remained standing. "Forgive me — I see this is a bad time — maybe I should come back when you are alone."

"What are you saying? Of course not. You just sit at the table, and I will bring another cup."

"Well, thank you, if you're sure," with an uneasy glance at Mama's friend. "I have to say something, maybe this German lady will not like."

My mother placed a restraining arm on her friend who was getting up. Then, turning to her new guest, "You go ahead and speak freely, Hannah Schmolinsky, nobody will bite you."

"It's about those terrible fights in the saloon about eight last night, when Mr. Resch was not there." She dabbed at her eyes with the napkin that was placed beside her cup. "A good thing my husband was not in there. He would have gotten in it too. One man got his arm broken. They took him to the German — excuse me — Lenox Hill Hospital."

"What happened — why?" Mama asked. "What started it?"

"Who knows," the lady shrugged. "They're still a little crazy, the —" with a glance toward Anna Wagner — "the pro-Germans, who forgot that they were in America," she added in her mixture of Yiddish and English, "and thank God, there are not too many of them left. Even the pros were mothers and fathers who had sons fighting in the war, maybe they got a klops for changing. Crazy people, instead of celebrating the end of it — they are stirring up trouble."

A silence like death fell upon the room. My mother's thoughts were upon my father whom she already saw with a bloody nose."

"Well, I must be going," Mrs. Wagner, visibly shaken, said. Our neighbor rose from her chair as well. "And I must — it was good of you to invite me. The cake was delicious. Goodbye, Mrs. Wagner, a pleasure meeting you."

Both ladies left, and Mama said she had a headache, would I clear the table. I said I would and my mother went to her room.

About six Papa came home.

He said nothing, though I was certain that he must have heard of that blood-letting in the saloon, but had decided to be quiet, considering discretion to be the better part of valor.

But this kind of evasion was not my mother's way.

"You heard?" she cried. To Papa's "what", she said heatedly.

"You know what. Those crazy fools starting a business there in Resch's place, when he wasn't there."

"Yes, I heard."

"Well?"

"What do you want from me? It was nothing. Just a little fight — they were all drunk."

"Is that all? Just a few people full of beer, bringing the police, breaking an arm; maybe they were not some left-over pro-Germans who got mad at the ones that changed? Maybe you think I heard nothing at my coffee klatch this afternoon from Hannah Schmolinsky?"

Papa laughed then. "So you know — but really, it's all over. Resch knocked a few heads together. There will be no more trouble."

My mother was not convinced.

"You will see," she warned. "They will not forget — I mean about the people who were opposite." When Papa remained silent, Mama added, "And who can say, maybe you will be next on their list!"

"Now you are talking like a child. Nothing will happen. Resch will take care of those people, if they do start anything, which I . . ."

"What can he do, I ask you!" my mother cried. "The war has changed everything. No one believes in the old ways any more. So, no one will believe Resch — with crazy people nobody can do anything."

The margin between sanity and insanity, in this post-war environment, was, as far as my mother was concerned, very slender indeed.

My father saw it differently. "I say, our landlord can do plenty. He is a big man with the Democrats. He will stop this foolishness."

"He said so?" Mama looked at her husband skeptically.

"Yes, he said so. And Resch is a man of his word. And you surprise me — can't you believe in anything?"

Mama said nothing, but her silence spoke louder than words. And with his own silence, Papa went into the front room. Over the whole house now hung an atmosphere of apprehension. After all, when all was said and done, what could our landlord do?

But, however it was accomplished, during that summer and fall, the mischief-makers gradually faded away. I believe the threat of banishment from Resch's saloon must have been the compelling force. But never again was it the street I grew up in.

Actually, there was nothing deeply rupturing, nor abrasive. Rather, there was unexpected withdrawals into homes, with excuses and embarrassed looks, when invitations were declined.

For my parents it was certainly a puzzle and a disappointment that the end of the war had not put to rest the arguments of the street.

How often had my father consoled Mama with, "You will see, when the war ends, everything will be the same."

Well, nothing was "the same". It was as if the prosperity which the war years brought had capriciously betrayed the old, pleasant ways.

"A new world is growing around us," said my father with a sad look. "A world it has become without warmth or sentiment and without the need for friendship. Never again will we see the old free and easy ways, of people with people, in close relationships."

Mama shook her head, "Yes, it was good to have a friend when the struggles in the beginning were too heavy to bear alone."

And she wondered, "How will it be, without neighbors to come to the door? Even now, it is already lonely for me, everybody so rich or so busy getting rich. My friend, Anna Wagner, she cooks for a rich family. She comes on her day off. Leah Rosen, from the top floor, sometimes she comes. But I don't know, it is not the same," Mama sighed. "My afternoon coffee, I don't enjoy it any more — so alone."

"And once we were like brothers," Papa said sadly.

"Well," Mama sighed, "this was once. Now the struggle is over. Everybody feels better if they could forget the old days. What I think is that we don't belong here any more. You know, it is sad that there is no longer the need for one another, as there was when we came here. With the new people it is not as easy to establish a relationship the way we had."

Definitely my parents did not feel comfortable in this new world they were faced with, where warm friendships were no longer cherished and held dear. When the last of the familiar faces was gone, it seemed time for us to pick up and leave as well.

And, as we emptied closets, shelves, packed barrels, every nook and cranny cried out with remembrances of the twelve happy years spent there, in the ups and downs of those early days, which brought strength and vitality into our American lives.

We moved in the summer of 1919, twelve years after that other summer that had introduced the Greenfield family into the new world of white sinks, gas meters and the immigrant affluence of the modern tenement on Eighty-first Street near the East River.

And as time whirled by, decade upon decade, there is still in my ears the sound of it, to re-live. Perhaps, for me, it is a Brigadoon.

**Books by German authors were burned in the wave of
anti-German sentiment.**

Madame Schumann-Heinck, a great opera star, had sons fighting on both sides. She symbolized the plight of the "hyphenated Americans." She was the best advertisement for the loyalty of German immigrants in America during the Great War.

Ten million men, many of foreign birth or parentage, registered for the draft in June 1917.

The doughboys
leave for France.
Two million troops
were transported
to Europe in
1917-1918.

Charlie Chaplin
and Douglas
Fairbanks, Sr.
(below), at a World
War I Liberty Bond
rally. Everyone
is laughing at
Chaplin's antics.

"All the News That's
Fit to Print."

The New Yor

VOL. LXVIII...NO. 22,206.   ....   NEW YORK, MONDAY, NOVEMBER 11, 19

ARMISTICE SIGNED, E
BERLIN SEIZED BY R
NEW CHANCELLOR E
OUSTED KAISER FL

SON FLEES WITH EX-KAISER

Hindenburg Also Believed to be Among Those in His Party.

ALL ARE HEAVILY ARMED

Automobiles Bristle with Rifles as Fugitives Arrive at Dutch Frontier.

ON THEIR WAY TO DE STEEG

Belgians Yell to Them, "Are You On Your Way to Paris?"

LONDON, Nov. 10.—Both the former German Emperor and his eldest son, Frederick William, crossed the Dutch frontier Sunday morning, according to advices from The Hague. His reported destination is De Steeg, near Utrecht.

The former German Emperor's party, which is believed to include Field Marshal von Hindenburg, arrived at Eysden, [midway between Liège and Maastricht,] on the Dutch frontier, at 7:30 o'clock Sunday morning, according to Daily Mail advices.

Practically the whole German General Staff accompanied the former Emperor, and ten automobiles carried the party. The automobiles were bristling

Kaiser Fought Hindenburg's Call for Abdication; Failed to Get Army's Support in Keeping Throne

By GEORGE RENWICK

Copyright, 1918, by THE NEW YORK TIMES.
Special Cable to THE NEW YORK TIMES.

AMSTERDAM, Nov. 10.—I learn on very good authority that the Kaiser made a determined effort to stave off abdication. He went to headquarters with the deliberate intention of bringing the army around to his side. In this he failed miserably.

His main support consisted of a number of officers, nearly all of Prussian regiments, who formed themselves into two regiments and placed themselves at his Majesty's disposal. To do anything with such support was seen, of course, to be Gilbertian.

During the night the Kaiser called the Crown Prince, Hindenburg, and General Gröner to him, and the consultation lasted a couple of hours. Both officers strongly pressed the Kaiser to bow to the inevitable, and Hindenburg informed him that any more delay in coming to a decision to abdicate would certainly have the most terrible consequences and lead to serious events in the army. For those consequences Hindenburg said he must refuse responsibility.

The Crown Prince, it is said, was the first to give way. General Gröner fully supported Hindenburg's view, but when the conference broke up the Kaiser remained unconvinced of the advisability of abdication. He is said to have come to his final decision an hour or so later, after several communications had reached him from Berlin and after another short and stormy talk with Hindenburg.

Meanwhile, his son-in-law, the Duke of Brunswick, for himself and his heir, had abdicated. "Brunswick's Fated Chieftain" was forced without fighting to abdicate. Reports have it that the republican movement in Brunswick, which long before the war was chafing under autocratic conditions, began to be noticed even before it was set in motion at Kiel.

Kaiser Shivered as He Signed Abdication

LONDON, Nov. 10.—Emperor William signed his letter of abdication on Saturday morning at the German Grand Headquarters in the presence of Crown Prince Frederick William and Field Marshal Hindenburg, according to a dispatch from Amsterdam to the Exchange Telegraph Company.

The Crown Prince signed his renunciation of the throne shortly afterward.

Before placing his signature to the document, an urgent message from Philipp Scheidemann, who was a Socialist member without portfolio in the Imperial Cabinet, was handed to the Emperor. He read it with a shiver. Then he signed the paper, saying:

"It may be for the good of Germany."

The Emperor was deeply moved. He consented to sign the document only when he got the news of the latest events in the empire.

The ex-Kaiser and former Crown Prince were expected to take leave of their troops on Saturday, but nothing had then been settled regarding their future movements.

GERMAN DYNASTIES
BEING WIPED OUT

King of Wuerttemberg Abdi-

MORE WARSHIPS
JOIN THE REDS

BERLIN TROOPS JOIN REVOLT

Reds Shell Building in Which Officers Vainly Resist.

THRONGS DEMAND REPUBLIC

Revolutionary Flag on Royal Palace — Crown Prince's Palace Also Seized.

GENERAL STRIKE IS BEGUN

Burgomaster and Police Submit—War Office Now Under Socialist Control.

LONDON, Nov. 10. — The greater part of Berlin is in control of revolutionists, the former Kaiser has fled to Holland, and Friedrich Ebert, the new Socialist Chancellor, has taken command of the situation. The revolt is spreading throughout Germany with great rapidity.

Dispatches received in London today announce these startling developments. The Workmen's and Soldiers' Council is now administering the municipal government of the German capital.

The War Ministry has submitted, and its acts are valid only when countersigned by a Socialist representative. The official Wolff telegraphic agency has been taken over by

Socialis

BER
people, t

Citi
with all
liquidat
a new t
public o
The
make e
the Ger
The
preserv
plish t
solve th
help.
I kn
have te
people.
In Germ
Therefo
for the
I de
know h
people,
political
supply
should
piles an
Foo
The poc
affected
supplies
their d
commu
and call

COF
cording t
lamation
filled.
Govern
the Gov

cers were
fired from
Reds ther
building.
killed and
officers su
When
the people
bank was
thousands

Times.

THE WEATHER
Fair today and Tuesday; diminish-
ing northwest winds.
☞ For weather report see next to last page.

PAGES.

TWO CENTS Metropolitan District 50 Mile Radius | THREE CENTS Within 200 Miles | FOUR CENTS Elsewhere

OF THE WAR!
OLUTIONISTS;
S FOR ORDER;
S TO HOLLAND

eals to All Germans
Fatherland from Anarchy

d Press.)—In an address to the
er, Friedrich Ebert, says:

rince Max of Baden, in agreement
has handed over to me the task of
er. I am, on the point of forming
the various parties, and will keep
the course of events.
Government of the people. It must
e quickest possible time peace for
the liberty which they have won.
n charge of the administration, to
ivil war and famine and to accom-
utonomy. The Government can
officials in town and country will

me to work with the new men who
but I appeal to their love of the
d in this heavy time mean anarchy
the country to tremendous misery.
y with fearless, indefatigable work
st.
In the hard task awaiting us. You
menaced the provisioning of the
on of the people's existence. The
ot trouble the people. The food
ther in town or country, and they
aid, the production of food sup-
wns.
e and robbery, with great misery.
and the industrial worker will be
lay hands on food supplies or other
means of transport necessary for
in the highest degree toward the

ve the streets and remain orderly

The new Berlin Government, ac-
ch, has issued the following proc-

people's deliverance has been ful-
'arty has undertaken to form a
ndependent Socialist Party to enter

'in the solution of demobilization
problems.
Serious food difficulties are expected in Germany, owing to the
stoppage of trains. The Council of
the Regency will take the most dras-
tic steps to re-establish order.
In the new German Government
there will be only three representa-
tives of the majority parties, name-
ly, Erzberger, Gothein, and Richtho-
fen, says a dispatch from Copenha-

WAR ENDS AT 6 O'CLOCK THIS MORNING

The State Department in Washington Made the Announcement at 2:45 o'Clock.

ARMISTICE WAS SIGNED IN FRANCE AT MIDNIGHT

Terms Include Withdrawal from Alsace-Lorraine, Disarming and Demobilization of Army and Navy, and Occupation of Strategic Naval and Military Points.

By The Associated Press.

WASHINGTON, Monday, Nov. 11, 2:48 A. M.—The armistice between Germany, on the one hand, and the allied Governments and the United States, on the other, has been signed.

The State Department announced at 2:45 o'clock this morning that Germany had signed.

The department's announcement simply said: "The armistice has been signed."

The world war will end this morning at 6 o'clock, Washington time, 11 o'clock Paris time.

The Great War
ends.

181

November 11, 1918.
New York
celebrates the
Armistice.

After the war Orlando of Italy, Lloyd George of Britain and Clemenceau of France met with President Wilson, to decide on terms for Germany. Opposition by European leaders and the U.S. Congress kept the President from his vision of a just world peace.

Woodrow Wilson sailed for Europe and the Peace Conference with high hopes.

Rejection of the Versailles treaty and the League of
Nations by the Senate left Wilson an embittered and
broken man.

Epilogue

Mama Crosses the Ocean Again

*T*he war was now behind us with the declaration of the Armistice in 1918. With my father's job at the Bawo and Dotter import house restored after the war, the pressure on the family budget was considerably lightened and my mother returned to her favorite topic of conversation — the possibility of a return trip to the old country.

When that subject came up Papa would always say, "Why not, if it would make you happy?"

My mother never gave a direct response. Always it was, "It would be nice, but —"

Epilogue: Mama Crosses The Ocean Again

Then, one day, papa brought the mail, And there is was, the letter from a cousin who wrote of the golden wedding anniversary of my mother's parents.

"Fifty years — my God, I can't believe it!"

Papa said, "It is a wonderful time for the family — all will be there to celebrate."

"Do you think we could?"

"Oh, no! Don't count on me. You go — I have no desire to relive my past. Europe for me is dead."

"Are you crazy?" Mama cried. "Cross the ocean without you — what will the family think. No, if I go, you go."

Papa remained silent. Suddenly Mama broke into tears, "Fifty years and no one to be with them of their children. I am here in America, my sister is dead, my brother in Australia. You know —"

My father said, "I see you want to go. Go with my blessings."

"Well, I would like — I mean, could we afford it, the ship tickets?"

"So, we will be a few hundred dollars poorer."

Mama laughed, "A few hundred! That's all we have."

"So," Papa said. "We will start over again. My job is steady — you go and surprise the old people."

"But I was counting on you — I mean, I can't go without you. What will they say? How will it look?"

"They will be so happy with you, no one will miss me."

"No, if I go, you go too."

"I am sorry, but believe me, for me Europe is dead. I have no wish to revive it." After a pause, Papa added, "You can understand, the unhappiness of that period —"

Mama shook her head. "I suppose I can manage by myself. All right. If we can afford it."

"The money is here — go and enjoy — with the blessings of our bank account."

Now, in our house, the door was open for all. Friends and neighbors poured into our front room where Mama had set the table with cups, cake plates, and steaming coffee. All day the well-wishers came and went. I remember a lady — a friend from the days on Eighty-first Street — coming with a package of gifts to be carried to her mother. "Since you are going to Yarac, would you take this with you? She lives in Novisad — she has so little." Yes, Mama was glad to do that. She would mail it from Yarac. With tear-filled eyes Mama was thanked. There were messages, more messages. Would she? Yes, Mama would. How could she refuse these people, when she was the lucky one to be going "home"!

And so it was that, after twelve years, my mother crossed the ocean once again. On a balmy spring day we waved Mama off as the ocean liner moved majestically into the distance.

To the end Papa refused to accompany her. Again he repeated, "For me Europe is dead. I have no wish to revive it." and added with a smile, "The happiest day of my life was when I landed here, in America."

Epilogue: Mama Crosses The Ocean Again

When the two weeks of my mother's journey had passed, the letter-carrier's shrill whistle was awaited anxiously by my father for news of "the family back home". Papa read my mother's letter with his morning coffee and added comments here and there. "Mama arrived safely, thank God," he said when finally word arrived that, indeed, Mama was happily settled in her girlhood home.

"You know, it is a great house, where your mother grew up," Papa said after reading the first news arriving from Yarac. "Do you remember it?" he added, and I had to admit that I did not, or at least only in a very dim way. "But Oma and Opa, I remember," I added hastily. "I wish they would all come here. We are so alone, and —"

Papa seemed surprised, "You miss them?" he said laughing. "You were hardly more than a baby when you came to live in their house."

"All my friends have aunts and cousins and . . ."

"Well, soon you will have your own family," Papa remarked casually.

Now, I laughed. "Nobody's breaking the door down." In fact, the following year I did marry the husband who is at my side today. But still, I missed the large family gatherings my friends enjoyed around the holidays.

Letters from Mama were less and less informative. They were sketchy and almost evasive; full of meaningless repetitions. "We are well — my parents are getting old. It was a shock, at first. I had expected them to be as

I remembered them. But they are old and bent and grey." Then came word of the family get-together for the fiftieth wedding anniversary. "Like old times. It was wonderful for the family to be together, once again like this."

But all through the correspondence there was something missing. Papa decided that it was time to face this point-blank. He asked, "What's going on there?"

This brought answers from Mama.

"The was has devastated the country. It will take many years, if ever, to get back to where we were. My parents are totally impoverished, as are all the others. But they are alive. For that we are grateful. With a sad heart I have to tell you that the big house where I grew up has burned down to the ground. This is what I was keeping from you. They are living now in the cottage at the end of the field, where the servant, Peter, and his wife once made their home. This is their home now. Beschke, Peter's wife, has died. Her husband, who had been with them since boyhood, is sharing their isolation. He is now more friend than servant."

Papa, in his answering letter, asked how they were managing for cash. Mama replied that she had already asked, but her father insisted they had enough for their needs. "And so," Mama wrote, "they are taking it in stride. Certainly they are not burdened by it. I was the only burdened one," Mama added.

Now there was talk of emigration to Australia "where we can once more be together." My uncle Erno had gone to Australia after the war. He was insistent that his parents join him. "We have a good life here. Australia is a beautiful and generous country."

But my mother hoped to take her parents back to America with her when she returned. Brother and sister tugged at their parents, each insisting that the two old folks would be better off with them.

And so the tug of war went on, with my mother hoping to have her parents with her when she returned.

But finally, both my uncle and Mama understood that Grandfather would have none of it.

"I was born here, I have my life here, and here I shall die," he made that quite clear. Mama understood that he was too old and set in his ways for a new start in life. Actually, my grandfather was about seventy-five at the time my mother crossed the ocean a second time. Everything is relative. Today, seventy-five is not so old.

"We have our roots here," Mama's parents told her. "People we have been with all our lives — the family — we have need for each other. Here is where we belong. The war years — we shared them with comfort for one another in our time of trial and sorrow."

The day came when my mother could no longer stay away from her own home. Papa had written plaintively, "You are needed here. The house has been empty too long. Come home."

And after aunts and uncles had gathered in my grandfather's place for a farewell dinner, Mama finally came home. The first thing she said to Papa after she embraced and kissed us was, "You know, now that I have been back in the old country, I can understand how you fell in love with America from the minute you came off the ship. Here everyone is the same. I never realized it until I went back home. Here no one has to be rich to wear a hat."

ACKNOWLEDGMENTS

I should like to express my appreciation to my son, Robert Jastrow, and to Doris Cook for their assistance in the preparation of the manuscript for publication. I am particularly indebted to Robert for collecting photographs that capture the immigrant experience and depict New York as it was in the years leading up to the Great War. Angela Kukoda provided valuable assistance to us in this photographic research project.

Many individuals went out of their way to help in the search for photographs of the pre-World-War-I period. I am especially grateful to Roger Whitehouse of Whitehouse and Katz, Design Consultants; Terri

198

Ariano of the Museum of the City of New York; Peter Dervis of the Bettman Archives; Anna Katherine Resch, my neighbor and friend of nearly eighty years ago, for the fine photograph of her father, Joseph Resch; Meredith Collins of Brown Brothers, who has been particularly helpful; and the knowledgeable staff of Culver Pictures, the New York Historical Society and the Library of Congress.

Finally, I owe a very special debt to W. W. Norton for launching my career as a writer at the age of eighty-two. I am grateful beyond words to George Brockway for his warm support of my first book, and to Donald Lamm, my current editor, for his continuing encouragement and personal interest.

PICTURE CREDITS

44 *and* 45	Brown Brothers
46 *and* 47	Library of Congress, Prints and Photographs Division
48 *and* 49	Museum of the City of New York
50 *and* 51	Library of Congress, Prints and Photographs Division
58 *and* 59	Brown Brothers
60 *and* 61	Brown Brothers
62 *and* 63	Library of Congress, Prints and Photographs Division
64	Culver Pictures
71	Library of Congress, Prints and Photographs Division
73	Culver Pictures
79	Library of Congress, Prints and Photographs Division
86 *and* 87	Culver Pictures
95 *and* 96	Brown Brothers
102 *and* 103	Brown Brothers
104 *and* 105	The Bettmann Archives
106 *and* 107	Museum of the City of New York
123	Museum of the City of New York
124 *and* 125	Museum of the City of New York
126 *and* 127	Brown Brothers
128 *and* 129	Brown Brothers
130 *and* 131	Brown Brothers
138	Anna Katherine Resch
140 *and* 141	Culver Pictures
142 *and* 143	Brown Brothers
157	University Microfilms International
158 *and* 159	The Bettmann Archives
160 *and* 161	Culver Pictures
162 *and* 163	University Microfilms International